We Live in the Mind

WE LIVE IN THE MIND

KGALALELO MPHEPHUKA

Reach
PUBLISHERS

ISBN 978-0-620-74421-8

Published by Author using Reach Publishers' services,
P O Box 1384, Wandsbeck, South Africa, 3631

Printed and bound by Novus Print Solutions

Edited by Derek Awkins for Reach Publishers
Cover designed by Reach Publishers
Website: www.reachpublishers.co.za
E-mail: reach@webstorm.co.za

Reach
PUBLISHERS

*Names and identifying details have been changed to
protect the privacy of individuals.

CONTENTS

For my parents, Tawana and late mother Mathota Saane
You gave me wings to fly.

ACKNOWLEDGEMENTS

I thank God, who inspired me to write this book and has been my constant companion throughout life.

I thank my beloved husband, Sabata John Mphephuka, for your love and support. I wouldn't have accomplished much without you by my side.

To my precious daughters, Botshelo, who allowed me to write chapters of this book at the time dedicated for her: she was only two years old when I began my writing experience, and Marang, who remarkably formed part of this journey giving me another wonderous experience – I love you very much, girls.

Thank you, family, for recognising the importance of this assignment and letting me be.

To my father, Tawana Bruno Saane, and late mother, Mathota Florence Saane, thank you for having chosen me to be your child and for the wonderful experiences we had together. I thank you, beloved parents, for having assisted and nurtured me to take up my own journey in life and for helping me fulfil my purpose. You did a fantastic job!

I thank my cousin, Tebogo Buntu, who has been my pillar of strength through the years, always ready to listen to my joys and frustrations without judgement.

My dearest Margaret De Koker, you have always been like a mother to me, believing in me and pushing me to be the best I could be. Thank you for having mentored and supported me with the utmost patience.

I wish to thank the Brahma Kumaris: World Spiritual University. You became my family and offered me the kind of spiritual support and genuine love I had longed for.

My greatest gratitude to Reach Publishers and the entire team for producing this work flawlessly.

Finally, I thank all the souls who have contributed to the experiences of my life, both challenging and magnificent; had it not been for you, I wouldn't have had a story to tell.

Thank you.

INTRODUCTION

In my walk through life, I came to understand, as I matured and exposed myself to many spiritual teachings, that our lives are ingrained in our minds. Our lives consist of the thoughts that come to us every day and the emotions that follow those thoughts. We perceive the world and everything around us with our thoughts, and decide how everything that we see, feel, hear and touch affects us. This can be challenging once discovered, and we might stay in denial for a while, but it doesn't change the fact that it is so. I have had the opportunity to live and learn, as well as to observe how others, particularly those close to me, live and conduct their lives, and realised that we all experienced the same things in life, but in different ways. Difficulties and challenges disguise themselves in numerous forms; no wonder the book of Ecclesiastes says: "What has been will be again, what has been done will be done again; there is nothing new under the sun." (Ecclesiastes 1:9)

What we experience is a constant repetition of events that everyone, at one point or another, has gone through and can attest to. The recognition of the power of our thoughts in our lives is startling and, even worse, how these thoughts shape our lives from the early years. I have also been the victim of my thoughts and those expressed in words to me by others, and all of these fashioned my life, but God has always been there with me through it all.

We are merely souls created by God and are on an eternal

journey of exploration in the here and now.

For me, life is like a screenplay; if only we could sit back with conscious awareness and watch ourselves act in the script of our own lives, we could correct every episode as we move along. We could paint the canvas with beautiful colours of our true desires and find harmony with everything in life.

If only we could think, create and act the way God does, we could have a real life, the one we were meant to have, and be what we were meant to be. This is, of course, possible if we are constantly connected to the mind of God. It is amazing to me how God has been called by various names in all religions or spiritual movements of the world, while the truth is that you can never find a perfect way to describe Him and His capabilities. All that I know is that He is all-powerful, He exists everywhere, He is all-knowing, He is within us and He loves us without any condition.

"For in him we live and move and have our being." (Acts 17:28)

We have been created in the persona of God and resemblance, and so God has given us the power to create and think as He does. We therefore are the carbon copies of God and have His full identity. We can, as a result, think and create with divine wisdom and reap the benefits, or we can think and create foolishly and suffer the consequences. God has given us free will, which is the ability of every individual to make choices without any hindrance or external force.

We have been fully empowered and equipped for the journey and it's up to us how we use the abilities and power we have been given: 'Safe to stick to God who is the Creator of man.'

There is indeed immeasurable intelligence running through the entire universe, and the book of Isaiah states it like this: "See, I am doing a new thing! Now it springs up; do you not perceive it? I am making a way in the wilderness and streams in the wasteland." (Isaiah 43:19)

God is always expanding and doing such new and wonderful things that the human mind cannot even begin to fathom and we cannot keep up with him.

This brought me to the conclusion that we, therefore, live in the mind, our world is in our thoughts and the only true thoughts are the thoughts of God and the true life is the life that God gives. Now, you may choose how well you live in your mind by the thoughts that you think and the decisions that you make in your life, or you may choose to live in the mind of God and do things the way that He does and emulate your Creator. Nothing can go wrong in the divine mind; everything is perfection! We have been created perfect and whole, but this can be difficult to grasp; it requires continuous awareness of our wholeness and simply living and being in the present moment. It also requires the constant healing of beliefs, conditioning and socialisation that doesn't serve us any more, and attunement with God.

I acknowledge Paul's statement when he said, "For I do not do the good I want to do, but the evil I do not want to do – this I keep on doing. Now if I do what I do not want to do, it is no longer I who do it, but it is sin living in me that does it." (Romans 7:19-20)

This book contains the story of a woman who has lived and still lives with the challenges of her thoughts and emotions, just like you, and has experienced and keeps on experiencing what you experience, too. She has lived and continues to live courageously, every single day confronted by all appearances of fear emanating from her thoughts and emotions, and still manages to reach her destination at the end of the day, safe. This is because she makes a decision every single morning to take the journey with her Creator and live in the divine mind, and every step that she takes is a step towards more life and freedom. That woman is me!

One teacher once said that whichever emotion comes up, it comes up to be healed and so we shouldn't despise what we feel but work at returning to the state of wholeness. My prayer is that you may realise that your thoughts are here to stay; you wake up and sleep with them because they are yours and you cannot run away from yourself. You only need to live bravely and make an effort every single day to unite with the divine mind of God and experience peace, joy and harmony that are yours by divine right. I often feel exposed and ungrounded when operating outside of God.

When you read this book, know that you are not alone in your quest and you can make it through any combination of circumstances that life throws at you, just like me, and achieve your goals and fulfil your desires. So, let us take this never-ending journey together and constantly rediscover ourselves. We wrestle with our thoughts; it's a fact; it is an unrelenting tug of war; therefore choose to live in the divine mind of God, let go and be free. Nobody says it will be easy all the time; some days are effortless and some testing; some days you will discover something new about yourself and think that you have made it only to find out that there's still more to see, know and learn. How far are you willing to go?

As will be seen in the book, I came to use different approaches in my personal journey that aided me at different stages of life. I come from a Christian background and Christianity has always been my base, although the circumstances of my own life led me to explore other ways available that assisted me in healing. I saw these as complementary, having lived for a long time feeling like a victim. When you meet someone in your life who tells you without mincing words that you are in fact responsible for your own life and that whatever happens to you is caused by you and by nobody else, you pay attention! It is, therefore, my viewpoint that there can be a combination of methods that would empower you and aid you; you need to ask for guidance from God in order to choose right, use discernment and clothe yourself in divine light.

14

I've prayed;
I've fasted;
I've meditated;
I've visualised;
I've affirmed;
I sat in silence;
I've journalled;
I went to church and other centres of spiritual learning;
I've attended seminars and workshops;
I've read books and sacred writings;
I've travelled and observed, and
I went to therapy.

God appeared every step of the way in my time of need and brought me people who assisted me, and still assist me at present, on my sacred journey.

Yes, indeed!

1

WHAT IS THE FUSS ALL ABOUT?

"Building a solid foundation in the early years of a child's life will not only help him or her reach their full potential but will also result in better societies as a whole."
Novak Djokovic

I grew up in a stable and happy home with both parents and my siblings, being the fourth of five children. I grew up with the normal challenges and joys of family life, nothing dramatic. The home front was harmonious, and all we children received the love and care that every child deserves from his or her parents. We would go to school every morning, and Sundays, we knew, was church day and Sunday school. I would say that the fuss began when my parents announced that we would be moving from a small mining area in the Klerksdorp district, known as Vaal Reefs Number One in the North-West province of South Africa, to Mafikeng, a town approximately 200 kilometres from where we lived, in the same province. This area had been my home since birth, and the significance of that announcement set in motion a series of events and experiences in my life that had the potential to mould me or move me in an opposite direction.

"Kgalalelo, please call your sister and brothers; your father and I would like to talk to you all," my mother called from the kitchen.

"Okay, Mom." I jumped off my feet to rush to the house.

I was outside at that time, playing with my two brothers; one was only a year older than I, and my little brother was three years old; at the age of eight, playing was a delight to me and a great way to pass time.

"Mom's calling!" I called to my brothers and my sixteen-year-old sister, who was keeping an eye on us as we were playing, and we all went into the house where our parents were patiently waiting.

As children, we were required to sit on the floor if we had been playing hard outside and it was only after a bath that my mother allowed us to sit on the couch. My sister, on the other hand, made herself comfortable next to my mother. She was neither a talkative person nor someone who spent too much time with friends. I guess, looking back, that was a bit peculiar for a teenager. She was a rare kind.

I still have fond memories of the red leather sofas at home; during winter they were as cold as ice and in summer I would feel the sweat running underneath my tiny thighs just minutes after sitting.

We had a large and spacious sitting room, and on the wall hung a huge framed portrait of horses. My mother has had that picture for many years and still does. We lived in a three-bedroom house, and all houses in that area looked the same and were the same size, as they belonged to the mine.

We sat quietly gazing at our father, waiting for him to speak as we knew that he would speak first as the head of the family. My mother was supportive of my father and never interrupted him when he was talking. We knew, as well, that whenever we were ill-disciplined, dad would know about it.

My father moved across the room, pulled out a chair and sat facing us.

"Children, your mother and I have decided to move to Mafikeng. You should start helping your mother pack, as we intend to move at the end of the year," my father said briefly and straight to the point.

My mother was sitting silently with my three-year-old brother on her lap, looking at my father whilst he was talking, not once saying a word. It was clear that, for her not to say anything, my parents had already talked this over and had decided. My brother and I looked at each other and really didn't know what to say, as we didn't understand much at that early age.

It was at that moment that my mother broke her silence. "Children, how do you feel about that? Mafikeng is a wonderful place and you will be able to see your elder brother and cousins often; aren't you excited?"

Our eyes gazed at our mother, who was smiling whilst looking back and forth at all of us. We smiled back and, looking at my sister, who appeared to be disturbed, I realised that she was not too keen to leave. She mumbled and grumbled next to my mother.

I got up, rushed outside with my older brother to continue with our play, and everything seemed normal to us.

My father had been offered a job opportunity in Mafikeng, his home town, a settlement located near to South Africa's border with Botswana and it seemed natural for the family to move over there as all my father's family members were living there, including my grandfather. My grandmother had died the same year in 1984 due to ill-health. Our grandparents lived in the rural village of Madibe, twenty-five kilometres outside town, and during school holidays we often visited with our parents. I also knew that I would see my eleven-year-old brother who lived there and had been raised by our grandparents since he was six months old.

Mafikeng was surrounded by villages and every time I visited my grandparents I felt as if I was being transported back to the olden days. Life was a bit slower and simpler in the village, with mud and brick houses scattered all over the horizon. The villagers lived by farming and you would see shepherds tending sheep and cattle in the fields. You were woken up by the rooster in the morning rather than the sound of traffic, and at night it was pitch dark as there was no electricity. We used lanterns and candles and you could easily step on the dog lying outside the door and would hear by the loud cry that you'd hurt it, as once happened to me. Although there was no electricity, unlike the urban areas, you could easily look past that and appreciate the intrinsic nature of the village life.

My grandparents owned cattle, sheep and pigs, and every morning my siblings and I would be called to the kraal with our stainless steel mugs to get fresh milk from the cows. We would drink it while it was still warm and unpasteurised and then run back to the house.

Our closest neighbour lived a few metres away in the village where my grandparents lived, and donkey carts were used to get to the faraway places. The villagers had land to grow natural vegetable gardens and fruit trees and build kraals for their animals, and my grandparents had a huge yard that served as an open playground for us every time we visited. I loved the contrast even at an early age and enjoyed every visit.

My parents never gave many logistics about the move; the how and the when were outside our scope of comprehension.

The idea of relocating sank in as days went by, and I felt excited every day. I asked my mother often if year-end was soon approaching and she would laugh and say we still had a few more months to go. Every now and then my parents would bring home empty boxes at my mother's request so that she could start packing up slowly. I would watch her on weekends in the kitchen padding her dinner sets and placing them gently in the boxes, leaving only the regular things that we used. She would then move into our bedrooms and start folding winter clothes that she stashed into the boxes as winter had passed.

It seemed as if time passed by too quickly up to the day that we left that December. I remember the day vividly. I was standing outside the house next to the garage, looking at people going in and out of the house with boxes that were loaded in the back of the truck. Our neighbours had arrived early that day to assist my family with packing and cleaning. My mother had done most of the work in the past few months and that speeded up the loading activity.

It was frantic at home, and there was no time for much talk, but only work.

Just then, my mother came out of the house and handed me the doll that she had bought for me for my birthday in October. It was huge and, with my tiny frame, I had to hold it with both hands lest it fell, and I held on to it until it was time for us to get into my father's metallic brown Opel Record. By noon, everything had already been loaded, and the truck left. We followed only in the afternoon as we said farewell to our neighbours and friends and took a final look at the house that was standing empty and aloof, as what had been our essence had been removed.

It was in an atmosphere of excitement that we children would take a long trip in a car, with the anticipation of seeing our relatives. We waved a final goodbye to everyone who stood outside in the street as the car pulled out of the driveway and headed for the main road.

The community of Vaal Reefs Number One consisted of mostly Sesotho- and IsiXhosa-speaking people. The cultures were diverse as the residents came from the surrounding and faraway areas to make a life for themselves on the mines. I spoke both languages very well at that tender age as a result of mixing with other children in the community. It was not difficult, therefore, to switch from Sesotho to IsiXhosa, and my family was accustomed to speaking Sesotho, too, though our mother tongue was Setswana.

Relocating to Mafikeng was totally different from what I had expected. We moved in for a while with our uncle who was living in one of the villages with his family, and then relocated to a house in the urban area.

The residents spoke Setswana exclusively, and the culture was of one kind – that of the Batswana people. Setswana was the only indigenous language that kids in that locale knew and understood, and there I was, a little girl from Vaal Reefs, speaking Sesotho to those I thought would be my friends in the new town. Being kids, they thought I spoke strangely and, since both languages sounded a little similar, to them it was a case of bad and broken native language. I didn't understand what was happening and felt like an immigrant in a foreign land, lost.

School was to commence in January of the following year, 1985. I was going to enrol for the Standard Three class as it was called at that time. I was thrilled to start at a new school with a new and different school uniform, but also apprehensive as I didn't speak Setswana very well.

That warm summer morning, after waking us up earlier than usual, my mother helped my brother and me wash and get dressed while my sister assisted in preparing lunch boxes for us which she carefully put in our new military green schoolbags. She herself had to get ready to go to a different school as she was in middle school, whereas my brother and I were going to primary. My baby brother had to stay at home with our mother until he went to day care. We left home and drove with our father to school that morning. When we arrived, the schoolyard was crowded with learners my own age and the beginners. It was the first day of school and parents were holding their children by their hands as they went to the principal's office for admission. We were all neatly dressed in our school uniform. While the beginners were crying at being in a strange environment, the old ones were running up and down, playing, shouting and laughing happily. As we climbed out of the car, an incomprehensible feeling came upon me. I felt fearful and overwhelmed looking at everyone around including the teachers, who were immaculately dressed with black blazers and were standing next to the staff office. My father led us to the principal's office where all the other parents were lined up. When it was our turn to go in, he spoke softly with the principal while we sat on the chairs, and so I couldn't hear what he was saying, but saw the principal nodding. He informed us that he was going to work and that the principal would take over from there, and then he left.

The school bell rang and the principal ordered one of the kids who was running around outside to escort us to the assembly to join the other kids for the morning daily parade. The entire school assembled every morning outside the school hall for the morning prayer that was rotated amongst the teachers.

At the assembly, we had to stand in rows according to our classes. The beginners were in the first row while my brother and I were placed in the third one.

The teacher who was leading the parade that morning started a Setswana hymn and everyone started singing. I didn't know that particular hymn and just mumbled along, trying to catch up as the others were singing. The hymn was followed by the reading of the scripture in the Bible, and then everyone prayed the Lord's Prayer. I was enthused, as I knew the Lord's Prayer, but could only express it in Sesotho. The prayer came to an end, and we all said 'Amen'.

While I was still waiting there in ignorance for the next instruction, it surely came. We were requested to stand still in salute while the teacher led us into the national anthem. Mafikeng was the capital city of then Bophuthatswana, a country that was separate from South Africa's pre-1994 first democratic national elections, when the country was then integrated into South Africa. We therefore sang "Lefatshe la Borrarona", meaning Our Fathers' Land. It was the norm to sing the national anthem every morning at the assembly at school, and we sang it with pride.

We were dismissed afterwards and instructed to go to our respective classes. I followed my brother as we went to the same block of classes that we had seen when we came in with our father; his class was next to mine, and I waved goodbye to him as I entered my class. I was surely nervous in the new environment on the first day and couldn't wait for the last bell to ring so that I could go home.

As days went by, I began to steadily pick up the momentum in class on the new curricula and even made some new friends; however, I was not out of the woods yet as I couldn't speak the native language, and I was laughed at every time I opened my mouth to speak in the language that I knew and felt comfortable with. My classmates were not merciful, and I was surprised at the amount of ridicule I experienced at school just because I didn't speak Setswana. Although other kids could understand what I was saying, they couldn't come to terms with the fact that I didn't speak exactly like them. I was appalled by their attitude towards me, and it didn't make much sense. Sometimes, I would laugh with them as they laughed at me and, other times, I would be angry. I was young and didn't appreciate being mocked.

Just when I thought things couldn't be worse, I was told that I was the shortest in the class. I never quite realised at that time that I was shorter than the other kids of my age. I had never perceived that nor was I consciously aware of it or understood what it meant until I was on the playing field. The teachers were no better; they aggravated the situation by sitting me in front of the class, and also moved me to the front row at the morning school parade. At my previous school in Vaal Reefs, I could sit and stand where I wanted to, and it was all right; it had never been a problem. Perhaps it was because my father was the headmaster, but I would never know. Like Adam and Eve when they ate of the tree of knowledge of good and evil and were thrown out of the garden of Eden, I felt exposed and out of place.

For the first time in my life, I began to feel conscious of myself and surroundings, something I never knew existed. I presumed then that my height and the language I spoke with its own accent were not acceptable and were a mistake. I needed to find a remedy for what I thought were disabilities. I began to read all the children's books I could find in Setswana, listened to my friends as they spoke, and in no time I picked up the language, became fluent in Setswana and mastered the accent. Part of the problem was solved, and I was left now with the stigma of being the shortest kid in my class and probably in the entire school; at least, that's how I thought of myself. I knew that there was nothing I could do about my height and so endured two full years of torment and persecution for my unfortunate stature, with no way out.

Our class teacher announced some time that we would be starting with the needlework and knitting classes, which would be an added period in the afternoon, and that boys would do gardening. It sounded exciting for the boys as they would spend time outside planting and watering the garden, whereas girls would spend the extra period in class. I was apprehensive as I doubted my abilities to know how to hold the needle, knit and crochet. We had bigger girls in class who knitted at home and when the classes began as predicted, I was one of the kids struggling in class. We had to show the teacher every time we finished a row of stitches as we had to make serviettes and table-cloths, and each time any of us got the stitch incorrect, we were slapped. I was a fearful child; I feared the loud and commanding voices of authority of the teachers, and would sit on my chair for as long as I could, avoiding having to show the teacher my work. It was the quietest class of the day as we had to concentrate. The only voice you heard was that of the teacher when she said, "Now repeat with the remaining stitches on the needle", and then we would follow her instruction and do what she said.

I abhorred that final period of the day as much as I detested corporal punishment and always looked forward to going home at the end of the day. We never had a culture of engagement with our parents as far as school was concerned and so I never even brought my work home for my mother to see. I would inform her only when I needed extra yarn at school, or money for the teacher to purchase materials for us.

Both male and female teachers were alike when it came to corporal punishment. We attended art classes on Fridays and, although the potato work was easy to do as all you had to do was to dip the half-cut potato that you had obtained from home into the paint and stamp it on a piece of paper, the authoritative voice of the teacher had to be heard, however, followed by a smack on smudging the paper. It was a horrible way to learn, although it was approved by the authorities. The final activity of my primary school days involved spending time with the singing class towards the end of the year. We had to compete in the interschool choral festival when I was doing Standard Four. All the public schools in town combined to celebrate musical excellence in a series of concerts that featured soloists and ensembles, singing a variety of selected songs that were commissioned by the school district.

Teachers who had a flair for music conducted the choirs, and we went for choir practice after school. I would arrive home exhausted in the late afternoon and still had to practise the notes. Getting them wrong meant an occasional smacking and, being a frightened child, I would practise day and night in order for me to catch the song and avoid ridicule and punishment. On the day of the festival, we were carried by the school bus to the event. The schools were arranged alphabetically on the stage and when it was our turn to sing, we sang our hearts out. Being at primary school, there was not much difference in tone between the girls and the boys, and we all sounded as if we were singing soprano and alto. The competition was, however, fun and entertaining.

My days in primary school soon came to an end, and I prepared myself for middle school with high hopes of a changed environment, attitude and new faces. I had thought that things would be better in middle school, but I was only deceiving myself.

I was turning twelve in the year that I entered middle school to begin Standard Five and things weren't showing any improvement. I had moved with some of my primary school classmates into the new school and they carried on the trend of mockery. This time I was not only labelled the shortest kid in class, I was told that I was fat, too. I had little if any recourse in correcting the state of affairs, and started to feel sorry for myself. I didn't know how to fight back to protect myself, or indeed what I had done to warrant such treatment.

I never told my parents or anyone at home about these experiences at school, and never knew that I could report the incidents to the teachers. I was teased almost every day and tried to avoid the culprits. I would change direction whenever I saw them coming and circumvented places where I knew they would be. I never even knew that I had shortcomings prior to my relocation. A cloud of sadness overcame me as I thought about what was happening to me, and the fact that I couldn't figure out what to do at that gullible age. I found solace in my books by studying hard, and that paid off as I was one of the brightest pupils in school. I had three years to get through middle school and it was a long and laborious phase.

Corporal punishment was a way used during our time to administer discipline at school. We were spanked when we made a noise in class, failed to clean the classrooms and the toilets, and sometimes when we did badly in some of the subjects. When I was fourteen, I had a maths teacher who terrified me. It was no wonder I did badly in maths, and even refused to take the subject in high school when I was given options. One morning, she came into class looking miserable and never greeted us as usual. She went directly to the chalk board and wrote a few sums that we had to decipher. She took a piece of white chalk, broke it into smaller pieces and threw it around on our desks. If the chalk fell on your desk, you had to go to the board, work out the sum and ensure that you got it right. We all hid our heads under the tables to avoid being hit by the chalk. We were scared of the teacher because, once you got the sum wrong, she would smack you on the face and humiliate you while the other learners laughed. I used to laugh at the others too, as they screamed when they were smacked. Mathematics was never an enjoyable subject as a result of my experiences with that teacher.

Athletics was also a nightmare for me as I was not good at it; we were punished when we refused to participate, and punished even more when we did. I simply could not run, I teetered and tottered and always came in behind. The teacher would come running after us with a stick, whipping us to make us run faster. It was horrible and I dreaded going to the field. The practice would carry on until such a time that the school was ready to select the best runners to represent the school at the athletic interschool competitions.

The ages between nine and fourteen at primary and middle schools were definitely the most unpleasant in my entire schooling experience, and that affected my self-esteem and confidence. I had been shaken so much in that five-year period, firstly by the kids and secondly by the system, that I was left perplexed. My father's home town had turned out to be horrendous. Well, I wouldn't have known, of course, how things could have turned out for me in Vaal Reefs, but I only knew things were not going well for me where I was.

I was left with the final stage of my twelve years of education, and that was high school. I wasn't sure what experiences I would have at that level; all I knew was that I had to finish my education to qualify for university entrance.

Surprisingly, high school was better, and I reminisce with fondness. Corporal punishment was still the order of the day, but the name-calling and ridicule subsided tremendously. I was recognised as a normal human being. My classmates treated me as a regular learner and no one made fun of any aspect of my being.

I did extremely well in my studies, and even joined a traditional African dance group as part of the school's activities. I enjoyed being in the group and was well accepted by my dance mates. I even began to lose weight as a result of dancing and, whereas athletics was still not my speciality, it didn't matter so much as I had found something that I enjoyed doing. We performed at all the school beauty pageants with our group, entered the local dance competitions, and even won a few. We were adored by the crowd, and it was a great and exhilarating time of pleasure and fun. My final year in matric was even more remarkable. I was proud of myself as, at the age of seventeen, I was about to finish my studies and the grace of God was with me.

We were in class waiting for the next period to start one morning when our class teacher, Mr Modise, came in and the class turned silent. "Good morning, class," he said.

"Good morning, teacher," we all responded.

Mr Modise was a soft-spoken man who was well-respected for his approach and we all liked him. We all stared at him as he moved towards the second row of our class, and I could see that he was looking at me as he was approaching. He got to my desk and whispered in my ear that I should come with him. I stood to follow the teacher as my classmates were glaring and gossiping amongst themselves.

"What have I done now?" I thought. Everyone knew that I was a well-behaved learner who had never caused any trouble at school. We all knew that whenever someone was called by the teacher it meant trouble was looming. As I slowly followed the teacher to the staff room, thoughts were running through my head and I felt uneasy. Our class was a block away from the teacher's lounge, so it took us a few minutes to get there. I could

see that Mr Modise was heading to the principal's office, and it made me jittery. He knocked on the door and I heard the voice on the inside say, 'Come in'. We entered the principal's office and, when he saw me, he smiled.

"Come on in, my child; I've been waiting for you, and good morning, Mr Modise, please have a seat."

I sat on the chair next to Mr Modise and waited impatiently for the principal to speak.

"You are probably wondering why I called you into my office, my child."

"Ye-es, sir," I said, with my voice trembling.

"Mr Modise, you really have a fine learner in your class. I'm impressed," he said.

Mr Modise smiled and didn't say anything.

"Well, the reason I called you in, my child, is that I received a call from the head of the Department of Education. He said that the television station called him about a show for young-sters like you. They want great learners, with good results, to take part in the high school television quiz." He coughed and reached out for a glass of water on his table. "I've looked at the mid-year results of all the matriculants, and you performed well; as a result, we have chosen you to represent our school at this show. This competition is open for all high school learners in all schools in the province."

Just then, Mr Modise interrupted, "We have looked at your track record since you began high school with us, and you have been doing tremendously well."

We received position numbers for performance during the mid- and final year-end exams. I had always received the first position in my class since middle school, in both sets of exami-nations. This time I had received the first position of all the matric learners combined. I was chosen to take part in the most popular television quiz to represent my school. I was elated, yet apprehensive, because the news came as a shock to me, and I could hardly believe what I was hearing. I didn't know that I had come out on top out of all the Matric pupils combined.

"You can go back to class, my child; there are things that I still need to discuss with the principal," Mr Modise said.

I stood, thanked him and the principal, and rushed back to class. I never said anything to my classmates as I was still trying to digest the news. I lost all concentration for the remainder of the day as I couldn't wait to go home and tell my parents. The announcement came the following day at the school's assembly, where the entire school and the teachers had convened. The principal broke the news and there I was, standing in the front row, smiling and feeling shy at the same time as everyone applauded.

I had a month to prepare for the quiz, and every day from then on I would meet up with Mr Modise during lunch breaks for thorough preparation. The quiz was scheduled during the ten-day school holidays to ensure that nobody missed classes and everyone would watch the show on television.

Time for my departure had finally arrived, and so I packed my bags and took my books as my father took me to a local technical training college, which was only a few minutes from the broadcasting corporation. When we got there, other learners had already arrived and were in the rooms that we had to share. I went to the reception area with my father to find out in which room I was being accommodated.

"You are in room twelve," the receptionist said. "Your room-mate is already there and has the keys," she added with a smile on her face.

I thanked her and said goodbye to my father as I hurried to the dormitory. The boys were accommodated in another block of dormitories and we only met at the dining area. We had a programme for the week, including on the day of arrival, and supper was first at 6:30 p.m. for thirty minutes followed by the rehearsal for the show.

We were all excited to meet each other as we were from different schools and, due to the condensed evening programme, we had to remain focused and remember why we had come.

A call came through the loudspeaker for us to proceed to the auditorium after supper to rehearse for the following day. We all got up and followed each other down the passage to the auditorium, even though some learners were not finished yet with supper and had left themselves no time. When we walked in and took our seats, the television producers wasted no time in welcoming us and immediately gave us the background to the quiz, how it worked and what was expected of us as soon as we were settled. We also had to understand the sitting arrangements as the following day we were heading to the studio for recording and had to be organised. The onus was, therefore, upon us to revise the learning material that evening based on the subjects we were nominated for. We were supplied with study guides to ensure relevance to the questions and thorough preparation. None of us had been on television before, and as a result, we were equally nervous. It gave me comfort to know that I was not alone, and I was even happier that I was not in the first round; that way I could watch how others responded to the questions and the method of questioning.

We spent nearly the whole night preparing for the show and none of us could sleep that night. I could hear a great deal of movement in the corridors; doors opening and closing and pages being flipped. It was a long and exhausting night, and in the morning we hit the showers, put on our school uniforms, had breakfast and went across the road to the broadcasting station.

We were escorted into the studio on arrival; it was dim and felt cold because of the aircons and we were requested to get settled quickly for the final rehearsal. The first three contestants were called to take their seats on the stage while the show host was occupied with arranging cue cards for questioning.

At last the show music began and the host took over. The

studio became quiet as we all sat in wonder and anticipation. We were all scared for our fellow learners, but knew that we were in a competition and the best person had to win. I was scheduled the same day in the fourth round which was the last for the day's recording and thought that, somehow, it would be easy for me to go through the show, but the experience turned out to be nerve-racking. By the time the host greeted everyone at home and requested us to introduce ourselves, I wished to escape but knew that I had to compose myself lest everyone laughed at me.

When the show came to an end and we went through the last question, I felt a sense of relief knowing that the following day it would be another set of learners.

At the end of the week we could have only one winner, and I wasn't the lucky one. The experience at the television studio was frightening, yet incredible. I didn't have the cheque or the trophy to take back with me when the schools reopened, but I had met some wonderful people and had made great friends. It was an experience that would remain in my mind for years. After a week of absence I went back home with mental fatigue, and I was happy that I had another week of holidays before the schools reopened.

2

A ROLLER-COASTER RIDE

"Intelligence plus character - that is the goal of true education."
Martin Luther King, Jr

I was preparing myself for school the next day when my father called us all in with the announcement that he had been retrenched at work and would have to look for another job as soon as possible. This time, at the age of seventeen, I heard the announcement clearly and understood what it meant and, being a teenager, it meant that I would probably not receive lunch money any more and would have to take a lunch box just as I had in primary school; at least, that's how I perceived it with a childish mind. Our lives had been blatantly interrupted or rather, the plan of a better life that my parents had contemplated having by moving to Mafikeng was crushed. The news came as a shock to the entire family, and no one could have foreseen the sharp turn of events. This meant that everything had to change; my mother was working in a retail store for a minimum wage and four kids had to be fed and clothed and have their school fees paid for.

Even though the news came as a surprise to me, my parents were remarkable, as always; they made sure that there was still order in the house and we were thoroughly cared for. I never knew how they did it, but, customarily, I wasn't one to ask too many questions. I only realised when I was sent to the neighbours for mielie meal sometimes that there was little in the house to go on. However, this is how many African communities took care of each other. It was the spirit of 'Ubuntu', meaning the spirit of compassion and humanity running through us.

My father looked for employment daily, and called all his previous contacts until he was finally offered a position in Klerksdorp as a primary school principal, and that meant that he had to relocate once again to a place that we thought we had left behind. It seemed the energy of the place was still with us and there was unfinished business that had to be completed there.

My parents made the decision that my father would relocate alone to Klerksdorp until he found a new home and was settled, and then we would all leave and join him. I didn't have the answers, and couldn't understand why life sent us back and forth.

We remained in Mafikeng with our mother and soon my sister and little brother joined our father, while my elder brother and I remained behind to complete our final year of schooling. Our eldest brother, who was living with our grandparents, came to live with us around that time. The parents tried as much as they could to normalise life for us, with minimal disruptions to our schooling especially, and so my father came to visit at every opportunity he got. His departure didn't have a huge impact on me as a result, as school continued normally and I was doing well because I was a bookworm. It dawned on me that despite the ridicule that kept me glued to my books during the lower grades of schooling, I had inherited the reading trait from my father because he was also a lover of books. In particular, he was a great fan of the James Hadley Chase classics. I came to love the series, too, as I was curious about what he was reading the whole day. He seemed to love his books, and I fell in love with them, too.

As for my mother, the job loss and relocation of my father

affected her health tremendously. I noticed that she was beginning to lose weight and was unwell most of the time. She had too much on her hands, taking care of three teenagers, ensuring that there was food on the table and still going to work every day of the week, even on Saturdays. She tried to remain strong for us, and made certain that we concentrated on our studies to receive good marks at the end of the year. She never complained about anything, and would normally go to her bedroom after work to rest a bit before she prepared supper for us. Her weight loss and constant tiredness worried me, and I decided to move my things to her bedroom so that I could take care of her. She was someone who didn't turn much at night when she was asleep and I used to wake up in the middle of the night and place my finger on her nose to feel if she was still breathing. I was afraid that she might die during the night and didn't get much sleep myself.

My brother and I studied very hard to gain university entry so that we would not disappoint our parents. We both wrote the Standard Ten final-year examinations in November of 1992, and as soon as we completed the final paper in the first week of December, the removal truck came again and this time took us back to where we had lived before in Klerksdorp. At this point, my family was relocating to the township of Jouberton, in Klerksdorp, and it was such an emotional time for all of us. It felt as if we were Israelites seeing Canaan for the very first time and feeling, 'Aah, we are finally home again.' When we said goodbye to our home and neighbours and friends this time, it was saddening as we were bidding farewell to a tumultuous life. It was certainly not the joyful experience that we had experienced when we first came.

We finally arrived home and were moving into a brand new house that was being built while we were still studying. We had relocated into a new neighbourhood and being together as a family was restorative, and so we were happy to be reunited.

It felt as if something had been broken and was now being put together again.

My brother and I stayed home with the family for the Christmas holidays, and then celebrated the New Year of 1993 together. We had to go back to Mafikeng, however, to fetch our results which were released just after New Year's Day.

"We made it with exemption!" we cried out as we held the phone together to speak to our parents. Despite the turbulent times at home, we had received good marks and our parents were proud of us. Things turned out to be terrific after all.

My brother and I took a taxi shortly afterwards and went home to our parents. I still had a few more days with the family before I could return to Mafikeng, as I had been accepted at the University of North-West to study for a BA Communication degree and had to go there to live with my uncle and his family for the duration of my studies. When the time came, I drove to Mafikeng with my father with a huge suitcase in the boot. He was taking me to his other brother's house a stone's throw from where we had previously lived.

I moved in with my uncle and aunt towards the end of January. They had two kids, a four-year-old daughter and a son, who was eleven. My uncle's daughter was such a delight to be around. I always remember her with affection, wearing a pink frock and rushing to catch the bus to go to daycare. She had very coarse African hair that resembled minute dreadlocks, and I thought it was cute. She loved sausages as a child and never stopped screaming when she demanded them. My two-year-old daughter reminded me of her sometimes when she was persistent about what she wanted; she also didn't stop until she got it.

The son, on the other hand, was at middle school, a loving and respectful boy. He turned out to be one of the most patient young men I knew.

I loved my uncle's family dearly as, through them, I learnt the value of complete acceptance of each other and of living together in harmony. My other cousin, Given, had lived with my uncle as well since she was twelve; she was my aunt's niece, and we were united perfectly, coming from different sides of the family. It was just what the doctor ordered. Given and I were both turning eighteen that year, just a few months apart, and we became the best of friends right from the beginning. She was easygoing and kind. We shared a room with a double bed, and the best time of the day was at night when we prepared ourselves for bed. We would have unending conversations about the day's events and the handsome boys we saw during the day. We developed a close relationship and were like true sisters, always doing things and going places together.

I was comfortable living in my uncle's home, as the only family I had lived with was my immediate family, with my parents and siblings. I didn't know that living with my relatives would be the same as living with my parents. Things were done the same way as in my own home, so I enjoyed it.

The schools reopened in the third week of January, and I still had a few days before I could enrol at the university. I was excited about the thought, being in a different environment and doing different courses from the subjects we did at school. I didn't know what to expect, but was filled with anticipation.

My father had to find the means for my first-year tuition, as I didn't have a bursary. He later told me, on completion of my degree, that he and my brother had agreed that I should be the first one to go to university for fear that, as a young lady staying at home, I might fall pregnant and never accomplish anything of value for myself. I felt grateful and moved by that gesture.

On the day of registration, my father came over again to ensure that my first day at university ran smoothly, and to pay my registration and tuition fees. Two thousand rand for registration was a lot of money during those times, and I couldn't trust myself at that time to handle that kind of cash on my own; I didn't even have a bank account. My father came early that morning. I was expecting him, and prepared myself for his arrival and the trip to the university. When he finally came, I was exhilarated to see him, as it had been a few weeks since I had last seen him. We got into the car and headed for the university, which was about fifteen kilometres from my uncle's home. We didn't know where to go for registration. I had only been to the administration block the day I had to submit my application form, and so that was the only building I was familiar with. We went directly to the information desk to enquire about registration and were directed to a huge hall not far from the main entrance, where registration for new students was taking place. I was excited, yet afraid, as I didn't quite understand what university life was all about and how different it was from a normal school. There were students all around campus, both newcomers and old-timers. Some knew where to go and some, like me, didn't, so I was not alone. The presence of my father, above all, made me feel secure. When we approached the hall in front of us, I saw a huge sign with 'Registration for new students' written on it. I was reassured, and my anticipation and excitement grew even more. As we entered the hall, I could see inside that there were some students in orange T-shirts, and it looked to me as if they were ushering. As my father and I were standing at the door entrance, unsure of which way to go, one of the ladies wearing orange approached us.

"Good morning, sir, and welcome; how may I assist you?" she asked, looking at my father, and then me with a grin.

I was looking around, not paying much attention to her, as I was fascinated by the movement of students in the hall.

"Hello, my girl, we are looking for the registration table for the BA Communication students," my father said.

"Sure, sir, follow me," she responded.

I could see that the lady looked older than me; middle twenties perhaps. There were about ten tables inside the hall, with signage for different faculties, and students were queuing at each table. I couldn't see where my faculty was. The lady led us to the last table, where I could see the registration table we were looking for. There was a young man waiting for us at the table who handed me the prospectus and asked us to find chairs and browse through it for the courses I was interested in. My father and I found a seat nearby and quickly paged through the prospectus to find the communication courses. I wasn't sure how to choose courses and which ones I was supposed to choose. There were many courses to choose from for the BA Communication degree that I was not familiar with.

With my high school mind, I knew that I would have to do a few subjects, and had expected to see biology and Setswana amongst them, but they where nowhere to be found. There was another set of people in yellow T-shirts whom I found to be the faculty administrators, and they were assisting students with the selection of courses. One elderly gentleman approached us, and I let my father talk. I was told that I had to do five semester courses with two majors.

I decided to major in journalism and political studies. I knew that I couldn't choose anything with figures, as I last saw maths in Middle School. English was a compulsory course for communication students, as well as public law, and I chose sociology as my last course. All courses had a small inscription of what each course entailed, and I felt satisfied with my choices. I wrote my courses down on the form they had provided and went to the queue to submit it. As soon as I had handed it in, the gentleman behind the computer punched the information on my form in the computer and gave us a printout of the courses I had registered for, as well as my student number. I actually had a student number! That really thrilled me. The gentleman told us to pay the tuition fee to the cashier, and gave us directions. My father and I went to the cashier's office to pay and, on my way there, I was smiling until we reached the cashier, happy that I was now a student at the university. I had registered for a Bachelor of

Arts in Communication degree, hallelujah! I felt proud of myself and was on top of the world.

The cashier gave us a receipt and a list of books I had to purchase to use for my first year at university. Whilst in a state of pure bliss, an announcement came through the microphone that orientation for the first-year students had been scheduled for the following week and all of us were expected to be there. We then went home to my uncle's, and my father had to go back to Klerksdorp. It was a sad moment saying goodbye to my father, but I was happy that I would be going for orientation the following week, and would be told when to start with the classes. My father finally left, and I went in the house to be with my cousins, who were watching television.

I woke up on Monday morning remembering that it was the orientation day, and I was keyed up. I helped with the house chores, took a bath, had breakfast and left. We were assembled at the huge hall, which looked more like an enclosed stadium. I didn't have friends at that time, and went all by myself and found a seat close to the exit. Some of the students started coming in and soon I was talking to the girl who was seated next to me. A tall and slender lady approached the podium, introduced herself to us, and gave a long speech about the reasons why we were there and the journey we would be taking for the next three years. She also announced that we would be taken on a tour of the university to find out where the lecture halls and the library were.

Now that I had met someone, we decided to go together. She introduced herself to me as Holly, and our friendship began as we realised that we had both enrolled for communication and would be attending the same classes. It was an amazing experience that ended at lunch-time. As I was about to depart and catch a bus home, Holly gave me her address, as she was staying on campus, and we began a journey of friendship together. The following week, I prepared myself early to go to class as the first one started at 7:45 a.m. I met the other students in class and made even more friends, most of them being boys. Classes were not the same as in high school, but I was coping very well, and did well in my assignments and tests.

There was a variety of extramural activities to choose from, and I decided to join the aerobics club to get fit and see if I could lose some weight. I had carried my weight consciousness to university and felt fortunate that there was something I could do, finally, that would help me shed the extra kilos, and that it had nothing to do with athletics. I went to aerobics every day after classes and went on the treadmill in the morning before the first class began. If I missed one of these activities, I would go jogging in the late afternoon when I arrived home. I soon discovered dieting pills along the way, and began to explore further and supplement my dieting initiatives. I convinced myself that, as a university student, I had to look good, and other young ladies like me were probably using dieting tablets, too.

As days turned into weeks, my desire to lose weight grew and turned into an obsession, and I became desperate. I wanted to prove to myself and everyone else that I could be thinner; I realised that my fat thoughts and the ridicule from primary and middle schools had in fact affected me. At that time, being as young as I was, I felt powerless but this time, having moved over from adolescence to adulthood, I was empowered to take control of my weight and do something about it. I would swallow a dieting tablet with a little water a few minutes before breakfast in the morning, which consisted of oatmeal and a bit of milk, took only a peeled carrot to class in case I felt hungry during the day, and would have a piece of meat for supper.

I ensured that I ate as little as possible at night, as I had been told by friends and read in magazines that food was not properly digested at night, and that resulted in weight gain. I was not prepared to be ridiculed again at that level and was determined to lose the weight and keep it off. One day during lunch-time,

I went with Holly to the mall to buy food at the grocery store. I bought a bottle of concentrated lemon juice instead of food, and squeezed it into my mouth, drinking half the bottle. Being thin was my goal, and although I wasn't sure what the true description of a thin person was, I felt I would know a thin person when I saw one, and I had to be like that, too.

I had never been a thin person since childhood, so this goal was the ultimate for me and had to be achieved. I had battled with weight in school and was never the right size, so the picture I saw in the mirror every single day depressed me. I actually thought that I would give up the struggle and accept myself exactly as I was, especially at that age, but it was awful when I saw the possibility of losing my childhood fat. What motivated me even further were family members, as they would always remark that I had gained weight every time they saw me after a long absence.

When people commented adversely about my weight, I would try another dieting method or a new product on the market. I would begin a programme, and then give it up a few days later when I failed to see the results that I wanted. As time went on, I began to feel despondent with aerobics as I wanted speedier results and never received the kind of satisfaction I was looking for. Eating less also didn't always help as at times it led to binging episodes and purging. I knew that what I was doing was unhealthy, but I did it anyway. After a while I discovered hot water with lemon juice, which had been recommended by a friend who told me that the combination helped combat tummy fat. I had as many cups of hot water as I could whenever I was at home.

Fortunately I kept a watch on my studies and the weight obsession did not affect them at all. I smooth-sailed in the first year and, in the second year, I received a scholarship as I had done very well and had applied to different sponsors during the course of the year. The sponsor paid for my tuition fees and provided the book allowance. I also began looking for a job as a student assistant in the Department of Sociology, since I had taken the discipline as one of my courses. Life was good as I earned five hundred rand monthly. For a student that was a lot of money. I could buy myself new clothing and had spare money to spoil myself with anything I wanted. The second year of my studies also went well, and I passed all my courses. I spent most of my time in the library studying as having a scholarship meant the world to me, and I needed to ensure that I achieved good grades so that I retained the scholarship.

I was at the library one day when Jakes came and joined me. He was in my political studies class and we were friends. He decided to sit on the other side of my table, facing me.

As we were studying, he suddenly whispered to me, "Kgalalelo, do you know Jesus?"

I raised my head and looked at him, perturbed.

"Well, yes, churches preach about Him - why do you ask?" I whispered back to him.

"Do you know that it is not enough to just know Him at church? You need to know and accept him as your personal Lord and Saviour," he whispered again.

I didn't know what Jakes was talking about. I was dumbstruck. He started sharing his beliefs with me in the library about how Jesus died for our sins, and the only way to redeem ourselves and know everlasting life was to be born again. Now I was lost and, all of a sudden, he said, "I want to pray with you to receive Jesus as your personal Lord and Saviour so that you can be born again and go to Heaven when you die."

I agreed that he could pray with me to accept Jesus in my life, although I didn't quite understand the full logic behind that, and I had never before heard about people being born again. Just to get it over with, as he was now keeping me away from my studies and disturbing my peace, I concurred. He then reached out his hand to me and asked me to repeat a prayer after him and at the end, said 'Amen'. He was done and could now leave me alone to continue with my studies. He told me that I was now born again and would receive eternal life. I never thought about what that experience meant until later in my life. I was nineteen at that time. I completed my second year, again with good marks, and knew that I was guaranteed sponsorship to finally complete my degree. I had become comfortable being at university, was familiar with everything, and even taught myself how to type quickly in a computer laboratory.

During the early months of 1995, whilst in my third year, the head of the department entered one morning and announced that the department was planning a trip to Atlanta, Georgia, in the USA, and a few students would be selected to go on this trip and to attend the 1996 Summer Olympics; this would also serve as an educational expedition.

All eyes were on the professor, looking at him with interest. We began to murmur, and he continued by saying that short-listed candidates would be invited for an assessment.

The 1996 Atlanta Summer Olympics were scheduled from 19 July to 4 August. We knew that it would be summer in the USA around that time while it was freezing cold in South Africa. Some of us thought how wonderful it would be to bypass winter at home and be far away enjoying the summer season. This was definitely something I wouldn't want to miss, although I knew that there were conditions attached. First, I had to be short-listed in order to make it to the interview and the assessment and then, the final results.

I was really hoping that I would be short-listed, and thought how good it would feel to go on this adventure and have that experience. I remembered my time at the television station, and felt that luck was on my side again.

The results of the short-listing came through the following week on the notice-board, and I had made it! I was exhilarated, especially when I found that my friends were also on the list. We were all excited at having made it, but that was only the first stage.

We prepared ourselves for the assessment that was to take place a week later. I wasn't sure how and what to prepare, as I had only been to one such assessment in my life for a scholarship and didn't know what to expect this time.

The day of the assessment finally came and we were handed the questionnaires. I browsed through the entire page in a few seconds and everything on the questionnaire looked foreign to me; we were presented with a long list of questions that required analytical thinking. I did the best that I could just to respond to all questions within the specified time, and a short interview followed afterwards.

I left the boardroom not feeling particulary confident about my answers for both, and consoled myself with the thought that at least I had tried, and now would just have to wait and see.

Holly changed faculties and enrolled for a social science degree, and so we were no longer attending the same classes. We saw each other infrequently from then on. We would meet occasionally during lunch-time or at the student residence where she lived. I liked her a lot as she was a cheerful person, always laughing. Our friendship faded gradually as she formed new bonds and I moved on with other students. We both had study time ahead of us and our interests had changed. I was grateful though that she was the first friend I had at university and we had had fun times together.

The results were due just two days after the assessment and I was very anxious. My friends and I rushed to the notice board again that day, and two of them had made it. My name was not on the list and I knew immediately that I wouldn't be on that trip. I was disappointed, but grateful at the same time that I was given the opportunity to prove myself. I watched as my friends jumped for joy, and decided to share in their joy and be happy with them. I had missed out on a great opportunity, but thought perhaps there would be another opportunity like that again some day.

At the end of the year I learnt that I had passed, and that meant that I would be graduating in April of the following year with my degree. I felt such a huge sense of achievement as I had never failed nor supplemented a single course. I felt like I was a genius in the making. The graduations were usually held in the huge auditorium, where registrations for new students were held. As a student assistant, I had served as an usher during a graduation ceremony. We had to ensure that the rows were correctly numbered and every graduating student was seated in the right seat. I had watched as all the candidates' names were called for them to take a bow before the vice-chancellor, and was overwhelmed with excitement that, one day, I would kneel at the throne of glory and have my moment.

I left for Klerksdorp in December to visit my parents as everyone was leaving for the Christmas holidays. I intended to return in January when the first semester started as I had decided to enrol for the honours degree. Christmas was a time that we all loved as it was bonding time with the family, and we were always eager to share the delicious eats that my mother would prepare. She was well and had healed rapidly when we relocated to Klerksdorp. She was happier and even regained all her weight.

My mother loved to bake for us and we all always went back with a tin full of her delectable cookies. She even decided to register with the Nursing Council of South Africa for an auxiliary nursing programme.

Time with my family was always fulfilling no matter how short it was.

I left home shortly after the New Year celebrations. My life and my friends were in Mafikeng and I had to get back there. I also needed to make the necessary preparations for registration and as soon as the administrative block had opened, I went to see the head of the Department of Communications to apply again for student assistantship.

The lectures began in the third week of January for the under-graduate courses, and we only began in the first week of February for postgraduate studies. I was now doing a lot of the research work and field study that I enjoyed very much. I always did well in my studies and considered that to be a blessing for which I was grateful. God had blessed me with the ability to do well in my studies, pass in record time and always come out on top. Studying was effortless to me and it was a natural occurrence.

The month of March soon came and the entire institution began preparing for the April graduation. The mood around campus changed as people showed enthusiasm and excitement in anticipation of the days ahead. My own energy also shifted, I was lifted and became light in my spirit just thinking about the ceremony. I couldn't sleep at night a few days before the gradu-ation because of the anxiety, and the clock seemed to be ticking very slowly. In a single moment everything changed and the day dawned.

The time that I had long been waiting for had finally arrived; I was graduating.

I woke up early that morning with a feeling of accomplish-ment, took a bath and put on my cream white suit that my aunt had designed for me. This was the prescribed colour for the occasion for ladies during that time. I looked at myself in the mirror and I looked lovely. I then put on my academic regalia and came out of the room to be greeted by my family ululating with joyfulness.

The graduation day was usually a day of festivity in my com-munity. It filled the town with jubilation. It was a time that we all loved, and candidates were allowed to invite four members of their families to the graduation hall to watch the proceedings.

My parents had driven early that morning from Klerksdorp to attend my graduation. As soon as they arrived, we all went together to the university campus accompanied by my second parents, my uncle and my aunt, and I saw pride in their eyes. I was the first child to graduate at home, and my parents were happy.

Lunch was prepared at my uncle's home after the graduation, and a few friends and neighbours were invited. I was pleased with myself, as I had fulfilled the vision that I had seen the previous year in the graduation hall. I never knew that what I had done was simply the practice of visualisation.

The day seemed to have ended quickly. What took months to prepare lasted only a few hours before the entire university and the community had to go back to normal. I had already started with my honours classes so it was an effortless flow from the graduation hall back to the lecture room.

The honours degree was just an additional year of study that I didn't mind pursuing immediately following the completion of my undergraduate degree. I had always been an enthusiastic learner and so continued with ease.

I was assigned Mrs Horns to supervise my research work which formed part of the degree. She was an elderly woman in her late sixtees, so I assumed, as she had grey hair. Quite a biased observation, you might say. Grey hair could have been in her genes but she looked mature in every way. She really wanted to see her students succeed as she paid attention to our work and monitored all that we had to do. She offered excellent guidance and practised tough love. I learnt so much from her and she wouldn't hesistate returning our work for revision if she was not satisfied. She was a dedicated lecturer and a former schoolteacher, and so she understood the learner behaviour. We all looked up to her as a mother figure too as she had the nurturing instincts in her.

I completed my honours degree successfully and graduated the following year, in April 1997, at the age of twenty-two.

3

A NEW ADVENTURE

"For no one can lay any foundation other than the one already laid, which is Jesus Christ."
1Corinthians 3:11

I decided to stay in Mafikeng for a while after graduation and look for a job. I didn't have any intention of studying further as I was afraid that if I became overqualified, I might struggle finding employment. Most of the job advertisements required work experience and I didn't have any. I didn't want to jeopardise my chances by registering for a master's degree immediately. I applied everywhere in the country during that period and in no way did I include my honours certificate. I was willing to learn from the bottom and work my way up. I noticed a few job adverts in the papers but all of them required three to five years of working experience, and that was both disappointing and discouraging. I had to find a job and I had to find it fast, as it was no fun being at home the entire day doing nothing. I had a friend in my street, Leonard, who was also looking for employment. He had a degree in psychology and was also struggling as I was. We used to go to the store together every Wednesday to buy the newspaper as the Wednesday tabloid had a special edition on careers. We bought only one paper and took turns paging for opportunities.

A few months passed, and since there were still no forthcoming job interviews, that resulted in me relocating to Klerksdorp to rejoin my family, thinking that perhaps I would be lucky there. I said goodbye to my uncle and his family when I left Mafikeng in June. I didn't know much about Klerksdorp, as I had only visited my family there during the university holidays and went back to university soon after. I also knew that Vaal Reefs Number One was a changed place from the time I left, and I didn't expect to find the people I had left there. I thought a lot must have changed in the thirteen years that I had been away. I hadn't seen my childhood friends since I left, and was certain that all of them would have moved too, and I wouldn't have remembered them anyway. I began my job search right away, and frequented the post office to mail my applications. I soon landed a job at the Edgars retail clothing store as a casual worker, working only during the weekends, although I was called during the week if they needed more staff for stocktaking. All casual workers had to wear black and white, which really made me feel like a penguin, as permanent staff had proper uniforms. I kept applying for permanent work and asked people if they knew places that needed new staff.

One morning, I bought a community newspaper and saw a job advert for a clerical assistant at the Traffic Department. I applied for the job, still not stating my qualifications, and was invited for an interview. A few days later, I received a call from the human resources department to say that I was hired. It was a permanent position, and I was thrilled to begin an eight-hour job from Monday to Friday. Though I had a permanent post, I still applied countrywide for a job I was more qualified in, and had faith that I would find it.

I sent out applications and remember being called for an interview in Carltonville in the mines. My father drove me there - I've always been daddy's little girl!

I was very optimistic and so was my father. Carltonville was not very far from Klerksdorp and I saw the opportunity of being close to home if I was appointed. The interview didn't bear any fruit though, and I was called again for another interview in Johannesburg, to which my uncle took me. I also didn't get that one but it was worth a try. I was gaining confidence in handling myself during interviews, which was a positive aspect for me; therefore I didn't see anything as a loss.

I enjoyed working at the Traffic Department and interacted with the traffic officers daily. I would watch as they had their morning parade with the chief of the department, did their salutation and then went out for their day's assignments. It was a fascinating experience, and I didn't have to watch it on television as it was right on my doorstep. I got to know Ariel during my time there; he was the entertainer and the comedian in the team. He had a very warm heart and wouldn't leave without going to the back office where all the clerical staff were stationed. We were four ladies in the office, capturing traffic fines that we received from the traffic officers from the previous day's work.

"Hello, my darling Ritha", I would here him say to the lady who was sitting next to me.

"Stop calling me darling, you know I'm engaged to be married," Ritha would say, laughing.

Ariel was very fond of Ritha and always dreamed of taking her out on a date. He knew that things were not going well between Ritha and her fiancé and saw himself as a suitable companion for her.

Ariel and some of his colleagues rotated the schedule every morning while doing the traffic report for the radio station for the Klerksdorp city centre. It was part of their daily routine.

My supervisor, Helen, enjoyed making fun of me also. She liked testing my knowledge of the Afrikaans language and would have a good laugh whenever I responded to her.

"Hoe gaan dit met jou vandag, Kgalalelo?" she would ask me

as she asked how things were going today, and waited for my reply.

"Dit gaan goed met my, Helen," I would reply, saying that all was well.

My Afrikaans accent amused Helen and some of the ladies in the office. They would crack themselves up whenever I tried to say anything in Afrikaans. I never saw any joke in it though, and the language has always been a constant struggle for me.

We also had to relieve at the reception area at times and answer the switchboard whenever the receptionist needed assistance. Mostly it was during tea breaks or lunch-time. I can't say that I enjoyed reception work that much, but it afforded me the opportunity to meet people, mostly those who came to enquire about their traffic fines, and others who had appointments with the Chief of Traffic.

The working conditions at the Traffic Department were pleasant and everyone was good to me, but I was still not satisfied. I felt that I wasn't doing what I was supposed to be doing and besides, I had just obtained a university education that I wasn't utilising.

A year later, on a Monday morning, a call was transferred to the back office from the reception.

"Traffic department. Good day, and how may I help you?" I answered.

"Hello, may I please speak to Miss Kgalalelo Saane?" The strong, powerful voice of a woman came through.

"It's her speaking," I said.

"Ma'am, good morning and how are you?" the woman said.

"I'm fine, thanks, and how are you?" I replied.

"I'm well too, thanks for asking," she said.

I was speaking to a Mrs. Lorraine Coopers, the human resources manager from a government department in Bloemfontein.

"Miss Saane, the reason for my call is that you have applied for the position of a communications professional in the department, and we would like to invite you for an interview scheduled for this coming Thursday," she continued to say.

"Oh, okay," I exclaimed stunned. "Thank you, Mrs. Coopers, I appreciate and accept the invitation," I said, with amazement and jubilation this time.

I grabbed a pen quickly to take down the details, thanked her again and hung up.

I thought about this for a moment. Although I couldn't remember applying for a job in Bloemfontein, I had been to Bloemfontein once when I was still at university.

We had taken a trip to a conference at Vista University with our sociology professor in my third year. I remembered that I saw a beautiful city, but never thought I would go there ever again.

I requested leave from my supervisor, Helen, for Wednesday so that I could travel to Bloemfontein, which was a three-hour trip from Klerksdorp. I didn't want to take chances and miss this interview opportunity.

I took a taxi to the town of Welkom on Wednesday morning, a trip that took two hours of travelling time. I had a friend I had met at the traffic department who lived there. She had come to pay a traffic fine and had found me at the reception area that day. We chatted like old friends and by the time she left, we had exchanged telephone numbers, and our friendship had warmed up.

Thuli lived in a flat not far from the taxi rank. When I arrived in Welkom, I looked for a telephone booth and called her to come and fetch me at the taxi rank. She was there in a few minutes and took me to her flat. She was still on duty and had to go back to work, and therefore left me alone to unwind at her home. I used the time to go through my notes whilst I was alone, and to prepare for the interview. I had the entire day to myself.

I spent the night at Thuli's bachelor flat. She gave me her single bed and said she didn't mind sleeping on the floor. We giggled for the better part of the night as we couldn't sleep. I was too anxious about the interview and relied on her to crack jokes and encourage me. The alarm went off at 4:45 a.m. and I jumped off the bed, nearly stepping on my friend sleeping on the hard floor of her bedroom.

"Good morning", I said yawning.

"Morning", Thuli responded. "Did you manage to get some sleep?"

"I don't remember falling asleep at all; I kept on tossing and turning," I replied.

"Well, you might need to keep awake with caffeine; I'll make us some coffee," Thuli said, trying to help.

"Thank you, let me go take a bath first and I will have some afterwards," I requested.

"It's going to be a long morning for you, but you had the time to prepare, didn't you?" she continued.

"Yes, I did, but you can never be too ready," I said.

"I guess so, but try to relax and listen carefully to the questions; you will make it, don't worry too much," she encouraged me.

"Thanks for the comfort; I can only do my best. Let's see how it goes," I responded.

Thuli took me to the taxis just before six o' clock and when we got there a kombi pulled over next to us.

"Good morning, ladies, where to?" the man shouted from the inside with the passenger window open.

"Morning, sir, I'm going to Bloemfontein," I answered.

"Hop in, I'm going there myself. Are you travelling alone?" he asked.

"Yes, I am, my friend is remaining behind," I replied.

I said goodbye to Thuli, jumped into the taxi and the vehicle sped off.

I was the only passenger in the kombi and took a place just behind the driver. I buckled up as the vehicle was going at a high speed. I reckoned that the driver probably had an early morning appointment in Bloemfontein too. I didn't complain though as I was anxious to get there before 8:00 a.m.

The driver was a very small man with a squeaky voice. I was surprised to see such a little man as a taxi driver. Most of the taxi drivers I had met were big men with commanding voices.

Our small talk ended there and we drove in silence until we reached Bloemfontein, a trip that took only an hour and twenty minutes. I didn't feel the distance at all because I was thinking about the interview most of the time.

I had to get to the address that was given by Mrs Coopers. I didn't know how to get there and relied on my companion for assistance. My taxi driver friend was heading in a different direction and had merely brought me to my destination, Bloemfontein! That is all he could do for me.

"You need to take a metered taxi to get there from the taxi rank, otherwise you will get lost; you don't know Bloemfontein, do you?" he said.

"Not at all," I replied.

He got off the kombi and met up with another man who was standing next to an old Chevrolet. I saw them mumbling as I was still inside the kombi. They both looked at me and came over.

"This man will take you to the address. He will tell you how much you should pay. My journey with you ends here, good-bye," the man said raising his hand and waved at me.

"Thank you for your help, sir," I said. I climbed out of the kombi and followed the other man to the Chevrolet. I never even got my companion's name but was grateful that he had helped me and had brought me safely to my destination.

The Chevrolet drove for about fifteen minutes and then pulled over in front of a huge building. I saw the sign in big, bold and visible letters, saying 'Lebohang Building' and I knew I had arrived.

"Here you are, madam, you can get off now," the driver informed me.

"Thank you, sir," I said with gladness.

'I'm finally here,' I thought to myself as I stared at the building.

I paid the driver, got out of the car and closed the door. The taxi left and I crossed the street to the main gate of the building. I stood there for a while, looking at the building with amazement, thinking, *'This could be my new workplace.'* I was still standing at the gate when a gentleman wearing a black suit, white shirt and red tie came out of the building towards the gate.

"Good morning, lady, do you need help?" he asked.

"Oh, yes, thank you. I have an interview on the third floor at nine; can you show me how to get there, please?" I asked.

"Just go straight through that glass door." He pointed at the door. "You will find the security officer there; he will be able to help you," he said.

I thanked the man and proceeded to the door. The entrance was manned by two security officers wearing orange shirts. I informed them about the reason for my visit and the one officer dialed a number on his phone, spoke for a few minutes and hung up. He then told me to take the elevator to the third floor and gave me the room number.

Thank goodness, I was alone in the lift and early enough to relax and calm my nerves. The elevator stopped on the third floor and the door opened; I took a deep breath and went out. I looked around but there was nobody around for me to ask. Fortunately the office doors had room numbers and I just looked for the number I had received from the security officer. I looked again to check the number and soon found the office I was looking for. I found a hefty woman at the desk that was facing the door, and when she saw me she smiled and asked if I was there for the interview. She had a list of all the candidates and she led me to the waiting room.

"Have a seat, Miss Saane, the panel will be with you shortly.

You are the first candidate," she said, and left.

"Thank you," I said rather nervously. I had thought that I had dealt with the anxiety but the closer to reality I got, the more panicky I became.

I was still sitting in the waiting room when I was finally called in.

The interview panel consisted of four people, the director of the Department of Corporate Services and her deputy director, as well as two officers from the Human Resources Department.

The nerves were getting the better of me right from the beginning and I felt that I wasn't articulating what I needed to say to the best of my ability. This was my first interview that was in line with what I had studied. It was my big break and I didn't want to mess it up. I received a lot of assistance, however, from the panel as they tried their best to calm me down and get me to relax.

The interview was an hour long and the panel kept on writing notes. I wasn't sure what it was that they were writing, and if they did explain in the beginning, I couldn't remember. I couldn't even remember any of their names.

As soon as the interview ended, I thanked the panel, then got up and left. I went out the same way I had come in, headed for the elevator, pressed the downward button, waited for the elevator to come, got in and went back to the security desk, where I asked for directions to the taxi rank. I needed to go back home as I was working the following day, which was a Friday.

"Go down St Andrews Street until the end; there you will find the taxi rank. You can then ask for the Welkom taxis. The taxi rank is not far; you can walk," the security officer said.

"Thank you, sir, I appreciate your help," I said with a tired but relieved voice. The interview was over and I could breathe again.

I was in my high heels and walked very slowly to the taxis. The rank wasn't far at all and I realised that I had paid a lot for a very short trip. I didn't know at the time, but the taxi driver obviously wanted to make money, and he surely did - out of me!

I took a taxi to Welkom again, and the trip took almost two hours.

I didn't mind that much; I had finished early and had enough time to get back home. When the taxi arrived in Welkom, Thuli was already there waiting for me at the taxi rank. I had called to give her the update about my trip, the interview, and when I would be back.

We went back to the flat and I couldn't stop talking about my interview experience and how eager I was to receive a call back telling me that I had been appointed in that position.

Two weeks passed after the interview, and there was no phone call. I worked as normal and kept applying for other jobs.

A month had passed when suddenly I received a phone call from Lorraine Coopers. I was relieving at the switchboard so I picked up the phone.

Mrs Coopers informed me that I was the successful candidate and wanted to find out when I would be able to begin. I couldn't believe that I had actually been appointed for a job in communication, the field of my study; it was incredible. I was so excited I couldn't wait to knock off and get home to tell my family.

I made the announcement to the traffic chief with the resignation form in my hand. Though he was not happy, he told me that he knew I was not going to stay with them for long as I was highly qualified for the job I was doing. I was grateful for the experience and the people I had met whilst working there. On the other hand, I was happy that I would be leaving home to be on my own and be independent. I had lived with family all my life, and it was time for me to explore being on my own and see if I could make it.

I left work at four in the afternoon and headed home for the big 'reveal'. I kept thinking about how happy my parents would be to know that I had been appointed.

I left home for Bloemfontein at the end of January 1999, to begin my new job on the first of the following month. I had worked at the traffic department for a year and a few months.

I didn't have a clue where I would be accommodated, as I knew nobody in Bloemfontein. Fortunately, a neighbour of ours had graduated at the local college there and hooked me up with some friends of his, who offered me temporary accommodation until I found a place of my own. There were three ladies living in a bachelor flat with only one bed. The situation was terrible, but I didn't have any alternative as I didn't know a soul there. Two ladies had to sleep on the bed, and the other two on the floor. Two of the ladies were kind enough to let me sleep in the bed with the other one. I was beginning to get used to having people move out of their beds for me; that was a good sign.

The best thing about that flat was that it was within walking distance of my place of work, and I didn't have to worry about transport. I lived with the ladies for a month before I was able to find my own bachelor flat in the same complex. With my first salary, I was able to pay the deposit for the flat and the rent. I felt a sense of freedom finding my own place and living on my own. I didn't have a bed or chair, but I loved the freedom, the peace and the aloneness. I slept on the carpeted floor of my flat for a month, as I intended buying a bed as soon as I received my second salary.

I bought the bed only at the end of the third month. It was my first huge purchase and unknowingly I bought it on hire purchase, thus ending up paying twice the amount. I was naïve and lacked information, making my first purchase mistake, but I promised myself it was also the last. I then chose to buy my next furniture cash as I felt I had been robbed by the furniture store with my bed purchase.

I started meeting new people in the block I was living in, and made new friends. I was thrilled to have some friends in the complex as it was getting a bit lonely for me living on my own and I didn't know what to do with myself. I didn't even have a radio or television yet. I would come to the flat after work, cook on a small two-plate stove, sit by myself, and perhaps read a book, then sleep and wake up the following morning to go to work again.

The weekends were even more daunting. I began searching for my home church, the Anglican Church, in the township so that I could go there on Sunday mornings.

I asked my colleagues at work and they gave me directions. I used the taxi to commute to the township where the church was and back. I went there for a short while only, before discovering another church which was a shorter commute and which everyone was raving about at the complex. It was a Pentecostal church and most students at the college were either members or sporadic visitors. I discovered that there was a bus that picked up the students at the college to take them there, and whoever wished to use the bus was welcome. Besides, the Pentecostal church was not very far from where I lived, unlike the church in the township, and so I decided to visit.

One Sunday morning, I took a shower, dressed up, took my Bible and went to the college, which was close by, to wait for the bus. A number of students were at the bus station, also waiting for the same bus. I was hardly ten minutes there when the bus arrived and all of us boarded, paid the bus fare and found seats. I didn't know what to expect and, therefore, didn't want to think too much about it and how different this church might be from my own church. The bus drove for about twelve kilometres and, as it approached the church, I observed that it was a huge building that was not built like the normal churches I was used to. The structure was different, more like a community hall when you looked at it from the outside. The bus went to the parking space allocated for buses, and everyone disembarked. I followed the others and we came to the vast foyer, where there was a group of very polite ladies standing at the door, uniformly dressed. They smiled at us and greeted everyone who was entering the church.

It was a considerable church, built in a theatre form inside, and it reminded me of the lecture halls we had at university. I had never seen such a huge church nor been in one before. I hurried to look for an empty seat, as the choir was already on stage singing.

The church was vibrant, and everybody jumped around clapping their hands.

It was nothing like the churches I had been to. Everyone was full of energy and looked happy. I had chosen the perfect seat, where I could see everything that was going on in the front. I looked around surprised, but sceptical on the other hand, and stood there surveying the proceedings. All the songs were displayed on the projector for everyone to sing along, and there were no hymn books. I was quiet for a while, feeling self-conscious, but on realising that everyone was unconcerned about what was happening around them, I also followed the screen and began to sing. I was content with myself as the more I sang and clapped hands the more the discomfort left me. People in the auditorium were carefree, with the focus on the choir and the singing, and absolutely not on me. The pastor of the church stood up and ascended the pulpit. He was a middle-aged man, charismatic, and he walked with humble pride, exuding confidence. I was captivated by his voice, which was authoritative. He requested everyone to keep standing and began to pray, and at the end the worship team took the stage again. This time I spotted in the group a medium-sized woman wearing a black ensemble, and with very long black hair. She led the worship song that followed, and her voice was absolutely angelic. I listened carefully and kept quiet; I was no longer following the screen but was magnetised by the voice. She was singing "On eagle's wings." I was captivated by the music the whole time and when the worship ended, we again took our seats.

The pastor greeted everyone in the auditorium and requested

the first-time visitors to raise their hands and be welcomed. I raised my hand halfway with hesitation, and was spotted by one of the ushers who walked over to me, grinned and handed me a brochure as he whispered, "Welcome." I was startled by the countenance of everyone there, which was truly amazing. People often say that things are too good to be true but what I was experiencing was real and very true. I felt loved and accepted as if I was a member of the church. Everything was organised, everyone who served was in uniform and you could identify every department of service.

I warmed up a little and continued to observe the proceedings when the welcoming was followed by the offering and, as the ushers stood to collect the offering, the worshippers ascended the stage again and began to sing. The lady in black yet again led another song. Her voice was delightful to my ears and I couldn't get enough.

I enjoyed the service and how things were done in that church, while the sermon was practical. The pastor used the stories in the Bible to illustrate the challenges that people go through every day in their lives, and advised us on how to overcome them. At the end of the service, we were all requested to stand, and the pastor then invited people who wanted to receive Jesus Christ as their personal Lord and Saviour to go to the front and join him in prayer. I remembered that as something that Jakes had said to me back at university, but this time everyone was invited. I saw people all over the auditorium move from their seats to meet the pastor in the front. The choir started to sing another song, and I stood there watching and paying attention.

The pastor prayed and requested all those who stood in the front to repeat the prayer of salvation after him. The service was nearly over as the new converts were ushered to another room for further teachings. We sang the last song before all received grace and were released. I jumped off my seat and rushed to the door as hundreds of people streamed outside. I had to find the bus I came with. I didn't recognise any of the people I had come with as the bus was full when we came; thanks to the efficiency of the ushers, the parking areas of the buses were arranged according to the different suburbs in the city, and so it was easy to find. On my way home in the bus, I kept thinking about what had occurred in church, especially the experience of accepting Jesus as my Lord and Saviour. I understood better what had happened in there than I did at university. I thought about the lady in black with the heavenly voice and how much I would love to hear her sing again. I decided right then and there that I would go back to the church the following Sunday just to hear that lady sing.

Monday came, and I went to work again. I was always hopeful that I would learn a lot of new things at work, but the experiences were not meeting my expectations, although I was glad I had a job in the field that I had studied for, and so kept my faith. At least I had something to look forward to: the church service the following Sunday. I was in such a hurry for Friday to come and go, then Saturday, so that I could prepare to go to church again.

When Sunday came, I went to catch the bus at the college again with the others. The bus came and took us to the church. I couldn't wait to hear the lady sing, and I waited for her turn to come. When it was her turn to sing, I would stand there in the audience and listen attentively. I didn't want to sing along, but to listen to her voice. I felt that if I sang along, I might not concentrate on her singing and would miss that voice.

I must be honest and admit that I began going to the church regularly more to hear the lady sing than anything else. I did enjoy the entire service but was magnetised by the voice of that lady as she worshipped beautifully. I began to really enjoy going to a Pentecostal church, and decided to leave my family church as I felt spiritually connected in the new denomination. My spiritual needs were met and I considered joining, though I wanted to be certain that I would be doing the right thing.

I continued to go to church every Sunday without fail and one day the pastor announced that there would be a half-night of prayer starting at 10 p.m. on Friday. I made a decision to attend, as I was in the rhythm of going to church and liked it. I knew the songs and loved them. The tunes were different, and every one was full of life.

The bus was also available for those services, and other people were even prepared to pick us up for the service if we didn't want to take the bus, so everything was made easy for us. We didn't have any excuse for not going to church and the night services.

On that particular night, the senior pastor opened with a prayer, introduced a visiting pastor and called him to the stage. He opened the Bible at the book of Acts and began reading the account of Pentecost where all believers who were assembled were swept suddenly by the violent wind from heaven as the Holy Spirit filled them and they began to speak in other tongues as the Spirit enabled them. The pastor raised his head and looked at us and said that those who wanted to receive the Holy Spirit with the evidence of speaking in other tongues should make their way to the front for prayer. I was still young in spirit and didn't really comprehend what was happening or about to happen, so I decided to sit down and observe. Many who came went to the front to meet with the pastor and as he started praying for them some began to laugh out loud and others fell on the floor. I perceived others shaking uncontrollably and I heard that they were speaking in strange tongues, but couldn't comprehend which languages they were speaking. This continued for a good ten to fifteen minutes and, looking around the auditorium, I heard people were praying in one accord with loud voices raised to heaven.

I was grateful for having been there as my understanding was growing each time I went to church since every time I experienced something incredible and new.

I was even beginning to understand the Bible better, and everything that was happening in church.

As I had accepted membership within a few months of attendance, during one of the Sundays I decided to receive Jesus as my personal Lord and Saviour publicly. This time I understood what that meant and was thankful for Jakes' introduction and preparatory stage back at university. I was twenty-six years old at that time; seven years after the initial induction.

On the same day, during the evening service, I also went to receive the gift of the Holy Spirit with the evidence of speaking in another tongue. I realised that to a certain extent I didn't believe that this could happen to me, too, and I was surprised. I gathered that God was and always is in control and He knew and always knows what He is doing. All that is divinely ordained surely comes and never misses its timing, and everything we ask of Him, according to His will, shows up every time. I believed that it was His will that I had to meet Jakes in preparation for the moment that had just taken place. The event at university had to assist my future comprehension and God knew all of that.

I began to understand Christianity better and lived a Christian life. Going to church and hearing the Word of God as it was preached kept me sane, grounded and focused, and I enjoyed myself so much that I attended church twice every Sunday, morning and evening, without failing.

I became more involved in church, attending intercessory prayer meetings during the week and Bible study meetings. I had joined a prayer group that met every Tuesday evening at a friend's house. We would go through the scriptures that the pastor had preached about on Sunday to help us remain spiritually attuned.

I remained motivated, and felt that my life was on course and I was living my life's purpose. Being in church brought joy and meaning to my life. I didn't miss home as much, as the church had turned out to be a home for me. I realised that one's family is not only the family of origin, but one can develop families wherever one goes. There are many loving souls everywhere who are willing to welcome you and treat you as their own. That is what church taught me, and I was delighted that I had chosen the right church.

I was cynical when I started, but now I was developing spiritually every day. I could relate to what was being taught in church, and there was a constant atmosphere of peace and love. I felt that I was experiencing true and real spirituality and left the church happy every Sunday. My experiences in a Pentecostal church set in motion a series of spiritual experiences that kept me glued to God. Whether those experiences were challenging or good, I knew where to run to for help and to express my gratitude. I continued to expand onwards, and embraced my journey.

4

New Learning Experiences

"It's through curiosity and looking at opportunities that we've always mapped our path."
Michael Dell

Work, on the other hand, was not satisfying enough. I thought, in my first month, that I would be exposed to so many things, go places and really get my hands dirty, but it was not like that. The pace was slow for me. I had too many expectations and was eager to practise what I had learnt at university. I was in a hurry to be involved in activities, but they were not forthcoming. Our division was new and we were the first three people in that new division. We had to start from the beginning and formulate a policy and strategy for the division without any base. I was sharing the office with the lady I was working with, and we reported to the manager, who was very quiet and gentle. We got along very well together, but I was not content. We had very little to do and would spend most of the time in the office with not much going on. Months passed and we decided to initiate projects to make our work more meaningful and relevant. We came up with a brochure that introduced the division and our functions, and then compiled all the projects that the department was involved in and informed staff members about them. We would visit different sites, write stories for the newsletter that we introduced and take pictures to accompany the news.

Photojournalism was one of the courses I had taken at university and now I was doing something with the knowledge. Our manager became the editor of all the print material we were assembling. We were beginning to use our different skills without being told what to do. We had waited for long for direction not knowing where it had to come from, but realised that we had the direction, we were educated, had talent and abilities and it was time for their execution. That was basically why we were appointed. We were all overwhelmed when we started as we thought we would have a mentor or be given instructions, but we had to instruct ourselves and take the division off the ground.

I also enjoyed inter-departmental projects where we would all showcase different aspects about our departments. Ours was a publicity stunt to tell people, especially the community, about the efforts of the department and how the department could serve its communities. I appreciated the motto that government throughout the country went with, 'Batho Pele', meaning people first. It signified the necessity of serving people, and that is what government is all about and what our department intended to achieve. I was delighted that I contributed to service delivery by ensuring that I, together with my colleagues, displayed the endeavours of the department to the public at large through different platforms. It had been a year and a half since I started working for the department, and I was at ease with my progress.

I received a call one morning from a friend of mine in the department who was the administrator in the office of the head of the department. Denise was a beautiful soul; we became friends from the day that we met. She was humble and a very polite person with a beautiful smile. Her positive energy was inviting, and I enjoyed going to her office whenever I had finished my work. She would invite me for a cup of coffee and, sometimes, we would order lunch and eat together. I preferred not to order lunch, however, but rather bring food from home as I needed to watch my weight. The thought of gaining even half a kilogram petrified me, so I couldn't take that risk. I had been dieting for too long, during which time I tried many diet products, but grew tired of them all, so I had to do something that I could manage and that was eating what I had prepared from home.

Denise was married and the mother of two small boys. She was the only one in my circle of friends who was married, and she didn't seem to mind at all having a bunch of single friends. I found it odd, however, for her to want to be with us as most of the married women I knew preferred to hang around with other married women. She later told me that she got married at the age of twenty-one. She had a beautiful marriage and a wonderful relationship with her husband. The only married couples I knew who were that close were my parents and my uncle and aunt. I didn't know of any others, especially as young as Denise. Her husband would pick her up at times for lunch if she was not lunching with us and I took pleasure in watching them together, loving each other. She invited us to her home one Saturday afternoon for a barbecue and it was pleasing to observe how she interacted with her family.

"Hey, girl, would you come quickly to my office, please?" she asked.

"Sure, I'll be there in a jiffy," I said.

I rushed to her office, as I was curious to find out why she was looking for me, and found her sitting with a newspaper.

"Hi, there, come closer. I want to show you something," she said.

I went over to her desk and she pointed to a job advertisement in the paper. "Look, they are advertising a job in the communication field; you might want to apply, and you have nothing to lose," she said.

I took the paper from her to read the advert that was in the local Afrikaans newspaper. It specified the required qualifications and competencies, all of which I had.

"Thanks, Denise, let me write down the particulars. I will definitely apply," I said.

The job advert was placed by a recruitment agency, and I couldn't tell for which company the agency had advertised. I rushed to the office to call the number I got in the paper, and the receptionist advised me to bring my résumé to their offices as soon as possible. I printed a copy and excused myself at the office, as I was in a hurry to submit on time. When I arrived, the assigned agent went through my résumé, and was satisfied that my activities matched the specified job description. The experience that I had gained in the department was paying off. I did enough for over a year to secure another job interview. I had chosen the right degree and things were looking good.

The agent informed me that she would arrange an interview for me, as a new person was required urgently at one of the large corporates in the country. The interview was scheduled a week after my preliminary interview with the agency, and I had plenty of time to research and prepare myself thoroughly.

The organization I was going to for the interview was within walking distance from where I worked, so I arrived quite early. I was ushered to the interview room, and spent an hour and a half being interviewed. The panel asked a lot of questions, and most of them required real examples of the activities I had done. I concluded the interview feeling satisfied with my responses and hoping for the best. My colleague in the office had also gone for the interview; hers was scheduled two hours before mine. Within a few days, I received a call that I was the successful candidate, and I was exhilarated, as it hadn't taken that long. I resigned and gave a full month's notice to begin the new job the following month. I felt blessed that I had been offered three jobs just a few years apart from each other.

I arrived at my new job on Monday, having been told to be there at 7:00 a.m. My new colleague had already told me on the telephone that my first assignment would be taking minutes at a strategic meeting for two days. I didn't have the experience as I was never required to take minutes at my previous job; we had the departmental secretary to do it. Martha was very patient and explained to me how to do it. This time, I not only brought my education with me but I had some experience to go with it that I had gained from my previous job and I had also gained a mentor. I knew that more was to come and that would only expand my horizons and advance me further.

Martha was the mother of two teenage daughters, mature, wise and in her fifties.

One of our job functions was to respond to media enquiries and to write media releases, all of which Martha taught me and showed me how to do. In my previous job my manager, being the editor of all printed media, would handle that function. It was really never a problem for me, since I was a junior and had to acquaint myself with other responsibilities. It was easier, therefore, for the manager to handle some of the more detailed and finer functions.

Martha ensured that I spent some time with her in her office, to assimilate as much knowledge as possible through watching her work, and then giving me responsibilities to fulfil. I had to report back on all activities she had assigned and had to justify my decisions.

She likewise gave me the courage to drive on busy roads. I had had a driver's licence for a few months but in my previous job I didn't need to drive much. Martha sent me out for meetings as much as possible with the company vehicle so that I could get used to driving in traffic. There were times when I would feel apprehensive, especially if I had to go to another city, but was grateful that through all of that I grew in confidence and trusted myself more.

I had sufficient work to do in my new environment, and every new day came with fresh activities and challenges. There was never a dull moment and work was by no means routine. The job was rewarding and I soon had things the way I desired them to be. I travelled extensively to some parts of the country and enjoyed each trip; I didn't mind going anywhere the company sent me as I was young, vibrant and still single. Sometimes I would stay out for two to three days working in another city and that was normal.

We received a call three months later from the marketing department. They wanted us to prepare a budget for the events we had planned to have. Martha gave the assignment to me. "But, Martha, I don't know how to draw up a budget. I've never done it before," I said.

"You should know," Martha responded.

Her response astounded me. Here I was, learning peacefully in a safe environment from my mentor and the woman I admired when things changed all of a sudden.

That is all she said, and she never uttered another word on the subject. I thought that maybe she had woken up on the wrong side of the bed that day. I left her and went to sit at my computer. I had to think really hard about how I could prepare the budget and present it to Martha perfect. First, I prepared a list of all the events we planned for both staff and the external clients and started thinking about how much it would cost to arrange the venue, organise catering, and the like. We had a filing system in the office and copies of the previous events were in the files. I took the liberty of perusing the files as Martha had a wealth of experience and had been arranging events for a long time. I used the previous events as the basis for my budget preparation and was contented to present my complete budget to Martha. She took one look at my budget and said, "Good job!"

Martha was tough and a perfectionist. Every assignment had to be detailed and had to be done right the first time. I enjoyed working with her; she had her moments like any other human being and I learnt how to approach her when she was in that space.

We were invited to attend a workshop in Johannesburg and had to take the morning flight as the workshop was to begin at 9 a.m. I had never travelled by airplane before and was looking forward to travelling by air for the first time. I had heard many aircraft stories of people becoming sick during take-off, and had imagined that I would also be queasy in the air.

I packed my bag that evening, and as I lay down on the bed to sleep I imagined all that I was to experience and felt satiated. Martha picked me up early the next morning to avoid traffic congestion and we left. I was overwhelmed by excitement and anticipation of the flight and the workshop. I knew that it was an opportunity to learn more and network with other people from other companies. We took off shortly after arrival at the airport and I found the flight to be a real delight. I thought my stomach would churn, but I felt peaceful and contented right through.

We arrived at the OR Tambo International Airport an hour later and headed for the conference centre where the workshop was being held. The first day of the workshop focused on organisational communication, its importance, and the different theories surrounding it. All attendees were communication professionals in their various organisations, and so we all engaged on how we viewed communication in our workplaces, and how we could improve it for the benefit of both internal and external stakeholders. The experience was edifying and it was pleasing to see both young and old professionals interacting and sharing knowledge the way they did. It was an intensive, participative session.

We had group discussions on the second day and the level of participation increased from the first day, with everyone being eager to contribute, and I enjoyed it. The workshop ended in the afternoon when we had to rush to the airport to catch our flights back home. I benefited a great deal from the workshop and would use the knowledge to improve my work - that was the idea after all!

We attended similar workshops regularly and subsequently I became better and better at my job. Martha had confidence in me and I was grateful for all the opportunities I was receiving and all that I was learning from her.

She was called for a job interview at another firm, and a few days following her interview she received the job offer. She resigned shortly afterwards and served her notice. I was sad to see her go as I had not only relied on her so much, but she had tutored me and cared deeply about me - I could see that. I knew that I would be on my own for a while until the company decided to appoint someone to replace her. It was not going to be easy or the same without Martha, since she had been a pillar of strength and was my guide. I had to assume the responsibility of two people in the section and do double duty. I knew that it was a great opportunity to prove to myself that I could do it on my own, and to see how far I could go. I took time to look at the files Martha was handling in order to acquaint myself with her part of the job, and felt confident that I would manage. I had to depend on myself and trust in my abilities.

I saw the reason for her mentorship, which was simply that I would be prepared to assume bigger roles when she was gone. I knew immediately that God had done it deliberately because He knew what was ahead and what He was preparing me for, and Martha was the catalyst to my development and advancement. She had been a soul who was placed perfectly to aid me on my journey. She had been a signpost, but her role had ended and it was time for me to fly on my own and meet other people, challenges and have experiences that would aid me further for more expansion. I acknowledged this divine collaboration and thanked God for Martha, for when the angel of the Lord whispered the assignment in her ear, she heeded. I had been designated to her and she did an impeccable job without complaining. I knew that it was difficult for her sometimes as I took time to learn some of the responsibilities, but she was patient and I now had to see how much knowledge I had acquired as she was released from her role of mentorship.

More training followed after Martha's departure, and from then on I had to travel on my own. I was invited to attend a meeting in Boksburg a few months later, and I took another morning flight to Johannesburg. The meeting ended at noon and it took me thirty-five minutes to get to the airport. My flight back home was scheduled to take off at 16:15 p.m. I tried to get an earlier flight as I had finished early at the meeting but it was fully booked, and so I had to pass time at the airport until it was time to board. I decided to sit in a coffee shop and have my favourite choc and chip muffin and cappuccino. Whilst there, my eyes fell on the display of the international flights that were arriving and boarding at that time. A desire to vacation overseas rose inside of me and I found myself day-dreaming about one of those destinations. I had a friend who lived in London named Fay.

Fay and I had met at a prayer meeting we attended in church and we soon took an interest in each other as we enjoyed similar things. She was a lovely being with beautiful facial skin tone. Her skin was as smooth as a baby's and her teeth as white as snow. She was engaged to Martin, who also loved God and was attending the prayer sessions with us. They had met at university and had been together for several years. Fay and Martin were married at a beautiful country lodge a few kilometres outside town, and I attended their lavish wedding with some of the members of the prayer group.

Martin had received a lucrative job offer in London which he gladly accepted, and he took his new bride and moved thousands of kilometres from home. Martha was gone and I missed her very much, and now Fay was leaving too, and, worse, was relocating overseas. I had been blessed with two wonderful people in my life and just when I enjoyed being with them, God had made different plans for their lives, and so I had to accept that. They say that people come into our lives for a reason, a season or a lifetime, and these two were definitely lifetime friends. Fay and I kept contact through email; we communicated frequently and she would tell me all about the new city she was living in and the things she was doing. She also had to start looking for a job in London to fill her own life and get settled.

The coldness of Britain was the only thing she complained about as South Africa is generally hot during summer and we don't experience much snow in winter. She would tell me that it had been grey ever since she landed in London and raining most of the days, and so she spent most of her time indoors. Her description of London captivated me and the life she was living there. I sent her an email to find out how she would feel if I visited them in summer for a week. I didn't want to go anywhere in the winter as I wasn't fond of the cold either. Fay and her husband loved the idea of me coming over, they longed to see someone from home, and the timing was perfect. I went to the flight agency in the vicinity to make my bookings. I had acquired a loan from the bank to pay for my flight ticket. I maintained that it would be easy to pay it back since I had a good job and no responsibilities.

I requested two weeks leave from my manager at headquarters and started preparing for my trip. When the day of my departure finally came, I took a flight from Bloemfontein to Johannesburg in the morning and headed to international departure with my ticket. I looked around for the London row, which I quickly spotted, and joined the queue.

"Madam, where are you going?" the voice of a man behind me said.

I turned and saw a Caucasian man next to me with a small sling bag on his shoulders. I could see that he had an official badge on his shirt implying that he worked at the airport.

"Who are you and why are you asking?" I responded with amazement.

He pointed to his badge and indicated that he was an official appointed to check credentials.

"I'm visiting a friend in London," I said.

"Let me see your passport. Do you have a visa?" the officer said.

"As far as I know I don't have to carry a visa to London, that's what my friend said," I told him.

"Well, things have changed and you have to carry a visa, otherwise you won't board that plane." He gave me a list of all the documents I needed to carry with me, including a recent bank statement, the invitation letter from Fay and Martin, and Martin's work permit.

I felt disappointed as I was looking forward to my flight that was leaving in an hour. The official informed me that if I rushed to the embassy and requested Fay to fax the necessary documents whilst I was there, I would be able to catch the late night flight. That gave me hope.

I left the queue to look for a phone and dialled London with a world call card. I explained to Fay what was required and, although shocked, she promised to fax all documentation right away.

I dialled another number to a friend, who lived in Johannesburg and explained the situation to him. In a short while he was at the airport to pick me up and rushed me to the British embassy in Pretoria.

We found another queue of people at the embassy who also wanted to journey to London. My patience was tested but I had to go through the process like everybody else. My turn finally arrived and I presented my case. Fortunately, the documents from London had been faxed, and Fay had called the embassy while I was on my way to explain that I would be coming and that those were the documents I had to submit with my passport. The grace of God was with me and everything went smoothly. I was granted a visa in no time and handed the copies of the invitation letter and work permit that Fay had faxed. I saw the hand of God in this situation as I wasn't sure whether I would receive my visa at such short notice.

The late night flight to London still had enough space for a few more passengers when I arrived at the airport. I produced my passport and my air ticket and rushed off to the boarding gate.

It was July, which was presumed to be summer in Britain. I had on warm clothes and a blankie since it was winter in South Africa, and that suited the night flight perfectly. I arrived at Heathrow airport the following morning and when I came to 'Arrivals' I started looking around for Fay, who was nowhere to be seen. I panicked. This was my first visit overseas and I had expected to see my friend right there on arrival. Other people came out, hugged loved ones with tears of joy and it was a nice scene to behold. I thought to myself that perhaps Fay had gone to the ladies' room and might be there shortly, but she never pitched.

I looked around for security to find out where I could find a phone and how to use it since I had to dial a local number. He guided me to a gift shop to purchase a phone card so that I could call Fay. It was quite chilly at the airport since it was still early, and I was glad that I was dressed appropriately.

I dialled Fay's mobile number at the public telephone and when she answered she informed me that she was still on the train to the airport and would be arriving shortly. She gave me directions to the bus stop by phone so that I could wait for her there, and then hung up. I immediately turned towards the security officer who had assisted me before to find out how to get to the bus stop, and he pointed the way. The direction was easy to find as the bus stop was just a few metres outside the airport.

Stepping outside the airport into the sunshine was revitalising. I was happy that I had made it and was not afraid, and ever since that trip, I have felt that I can go anywhere in the world as God was always with me and would see me through. God never leaves us alone without any help, I learnt from that trip. Even though I nearly didn't make it to London as a result of a lack of documentation, He provided and opened doors, ensuring that I met the new flight schedule. My missing the earlier flight to Bloemfontein after the Boksburg meeting and ending up seeing Heathrow airport on the board was no accident. It was divinely planned like any of my life's events.

Fay came just a few minutes later and I was relieved and happy to see her. We boarded the bus to Croydon, which was quite a distance from the airport. It could have been that I was not used to travelling that far as I come from a small town and the airport was not too far away. We chatted on the way and I was eager to hear how life was in London for her. The greyness that she spoke about, well, I have experienced it and, although it was supposed to be summer, I felt cold. I spent a week in London with Fay and Martin, and they took me to many interesting places, which was kind of them. The day I arrived we went to visit their friends in the evening for a prayer group meeting at eight o' clock, and I was surprised that it was not dark as yet. It was only two hours later that darkness fell on the city, and my body couldn't cope well as I was exhausted from the trip itself, and at home I'm usually fast asleep at ten o'clock every night. I was desperate to go to bed.

London is widely known for its excellent transportation system. Getting everywhere from anywhere was extremely easy. You would find a bus at every corner and the underground railway system was quick. We went everywhere on public transport and I enjoyed every minute of it. I discovered my love for observing phenomena and just the movement of people all around. We would at times walk long distances to get to the train station, depending on where Fay and Martin were taking me for the day, and all of that was quite satisfying. Flat shoes were all that was required of me. It was a fulfilling week for me, and I have since discovered that a week is usually enough time for me to be away.

I flew back home on a Saturday and it was a long eleven hours non-stop flight from Heathrow to Johannesburg. It felt quicker when I left because of the anticipation, but longer when I returned, and even the movies that I watched on board couldn't satisfy the desire to be home in a short period of time. On my arrival in Johannesburg I took an exchange flight to Bloemfontein of just an hour. I arrived home exhausted and jumped into the shower.

I still had another day of rest on Sunday before going back to work. I slept for the better part of the day as I knew what was awaiting me the following day at work.

Since Martha had gone, I continued to work alone in my department and nothing was said about the appointment of another person to assist me. There were days that were challenging while others came easy, and there were times during the hectic days were I felt overwhelmed and unsure of myself. I had to work very hard so that I wouldn't disappoint myself and Martha. We kept in touch by telephone and whenever I got stuck and felt uncertain about any activity, she would guide me. Martha became more than just a friend to me, she was like a mother to the extent that even when I had personal problems I would call her and she always knew what to say to make me feel better. I never could forget her and we became even closer when she was not around. Her move was for her good and her own growth. She was a spiritual woman herself, and I guess that's what made us click and grow closer. We kept each other in prayer all the time.

I developed every day in my job and was confident enough to make effective changes to enhance the division. I only had to give feedback in the form of weekly reports to my manager, and I never received any complaints.

5

A Spiritual Journey with a Twist

"Our life's path is revealed to us by spiritual guideposts. They mark the way and lead us to our soul's ultimate purpose."
Randi G Fine

I continued to go to church every Sunday, attending prayer meetings on Tuesdays and the Fridays' half-night prayers whenever they were arranged. I also continued to go to work as usual, doing it the best way I could and going home afterwards feeling exhausted. I had been going to the new church for a year now, while Martha had been gone for some time, although we still kept in contact, and I had frequent conversations with Fay about matters of the spirit. We would write long emails to each other questioning the conduct in some of the churches and sometimes what we were taught. We were both maturing spiritually and reading many Christian books to expand our knowledge and engage even more. Some of the teachings challenged me personally, and with my enquiring mind I began to do more research while seeking more information.

I also began re-evaluating my entire life and wondered if something was missing. I felt empty inside at times and couldn't quite pin it on anything specific. I had a townhouse, a car, beautiful clothes and the normal things that everyone had, things that society believed brought happiness, but I felt a void in my soul.

The previous year I had believed that I had a purpose in my life and that my life had meaning, but all of a sudden I had a vacuum in my heart and couldn't explain the rationale. Then again, my friends were getting married and having children, and so I wondered if that was it, but I wasn't sure.

I spent more time on my own trying to figure out why I was feeling the way I did, but I couldn't find the answers. I looked at my job, thinking it was a contributing factor, but I still didn't have clarity. At times I would reason that perhaps I was feeling lonely because I was losing friends who were dear to me. Just as I was thinking that things could not get any worse, Denise and her husband also moved. Her husband had received a promotion to another company in Johannesburg and that forced Denise also to resign as they needed to find a new school for the kids.

I found myself in a state of bewilderment and thrown into disarray. The ground that I was walking on was shaky. I began receiving even more wedding invitations and almost every week a wedding would be announced in church.

"Am I missing out on this?" I asked myself. I knew, though, that I wanted to be married and have children some day, and to have a beautiful wedding. After all, the thought was planted in my mind. I had already thought of the theme too, and that would be gold and white, but the timing was not right. I was dating a carefree man who adored his friends and partied most of the time, and I was certain that marriage was far from his mind.

I remembered that my prayer group leader had once said that most women obsess about having a wedding instead of thinking about marriage. He pointed out that a wedding was a ceremony of getting married whereas the marriage itself was a long-term commitment between two people and that love had to be at the centre of that union.

He said that more work was required to cultivate a marriage than to plan a wedding, but people usually had things the other way round. They focused on the day of their wedding and how beautiful the occasion would be, the flowers, the dress and the cake, instead of focusing ahead on the other side of the big day.

This rang true for me as most of the ladies I met in church spoke about nothing but weddings, and I also noticed that getting married was emphasised more often than not in the church. The emphasis was not necessarily from the senior pastor, although sometimes he did encourage people to get married to avoid falling into temptation, but mostly it came from the congregants themselves and the prayer group leaders. This portrayed marriage for me as if it was all there was in life, and nothing else. You had to get married and have children and live happily ever after. The equation didn't sound right to me as I didn't believe that this was the square of life; getting married and having children, of course, was part of the equation but not the entire picture.

I had been to a wedding of a friend whose fiancé had forgotten the bow tie at home. My friend was worked up as she wanted everything to be perfect and the bow tie was needed to complete the dream wedding picture. The best man had to be sent back before the wedding ceremony could begin to fetch the small black bow tie. I thought it was really funny how everybody got worked up to fulfil a wedding fantasy. The pictures wouldn't have been complete without the tiny little bow tie in the maze!

I was not going to put my life on hold though, waiting for a wedding, or rather marriage. A male friend of mine once said that flowers don't chase bees, but bees find their flowers and I knew that I had to wait for the right time if indeed marriage was the missing piece of the puzzle.

In the meantime, I had to get to the source of displeasure about my life and look at all the areas.

I began visiting the local bookshop at the mall on Saturdays and, somehow, would end up at the psychology as well as the mind, body and spirit bookshelves. I didn't have friends to hang around with any more during weekends, so I went solo. I needed to find a different perspective, and during one of my visits I found a book by Louise L. Hay titled 'You can heal your life'. I wanted to discover what it was about my life that needed healing and how to fill the vacuum I was feeling deep inside, and this seemed like the right title.

I took the book from the shelf and found a seat in the aisle. The bookshop allowed us to read for a little while if we wanted to, and provided a few chairs next to the shelves. I quickly paged through the book and was intrigued by what I read. The book explained that all emotional difficulties and illnesses in our bodies emanated from a lack of self-love. If we love, approve and appreciate ourselves completely we will alleviate all the negativity that has a harmful effect on our entire being. Our thought patterns are at the centre of this negative energy, and if we can change our thoughts and beliefs about ourselves, we can live happier lives. Hay also highlighted that self-criticism and self-doubt were our enemies and if we loved ourselves perfectly, self-judgement would fade away. I thought about her words for a moment and asked myself whether I was bashing myself all the time, and realised that this was true and that according to the author this was not an act of love.

I also thought about the scriptures that said: "perfect love drives out fear, because fear has to do with punishment," (1 John 4:18) and that there is "no condemnation for those who are in Christ Jesus." (Romans 8:1)

With my self-enquiry I realised that I wanted to be the best at what I did, especially at work, and therefore I worked hard to reach my goals. I saw clearly that I often criticized myself if there was an activity I couldn't complete to perfection.

I also enjoyed having friends and felt alone if they were not around. I would drive around town not knowing where to go because I felt bored. I simply didn't enjoy my own company. I also felt happy when my boyfriend was around, and if he couldn't make it that was a problem for me. I wanted to be a perfect prayer warrior and pray the way I heard 'church' people prayed, phrase my words the way they did in prayer, quote the perfect scriptures, worship the way others did and act the way 'church' people were supposed to act, especially being a born-again Christian. I still wanted to lose weight and was constantly on a diet. I had been on a diet since I was eighteen years old, beginning in my first year at university. I cannot remember the time that I was not on a diet. I could never just accept myself the way that I was; my body, my shape, my curves and the entire African in me.

It was indeed true that I wasn't giving myself the love that I wanted in my life but depended on others to love and care for me in order to fill my life. I depended on others' compliments to me without complimenting myself. They had to tell me that I looked and was beautiful, and I couldn't do that myself because I didn't believe that I was good enough the way that I was. This was scary but true. The words of the author liberated me; I had read only a few pages and decided to buy the book to read it further at home. She had introduced me to the concept of affirmations, that I could affirm out loud the results I wanted to see in my life. I found the concept appealing and another method I could use to find peace and joy in my life. I took the book with me and stood at the counter to pay for it.

As I was paying, my eyes fell on the magazine stand nearby and I saw a magazine with the title 'Mind, body and spirit', which I took and paid for as well. It was satisfying for me that I had found a book that I wanted, and then a magazine that could contain some of the things that might interest me, as well. It was certainly not a coincidence.

I left the mall in a hurry and drove home whilst meditating on the few paragraphs I had read from the book. My mind shifted to all my encounters with spirituality, first from Sunday school, my family church, Jakes and the Pentecostal church I was attending at that time. I had thought that, as far as spirituality was concerned, I knew it all, but still I couldn't understand and explain the emptiness I was constantly feeling. I thought the material things I had were the alpha and the omega and what everyone aspired to have in life. Perhaps I needed the more refined versions of what I had. I tried to come up with reasons that I thought made sense, but knew that there was something deeper than just having things.

I arrived home just after the lunch hour and started reading the book. It was captivating, and I underlined some of the statements that rang true for me. I was not familiar with the author's style of writing. Her emphasis was on the science of the mind; she explained the thought process and how we create everything in our lives with our thoughts. I paused and took a big breath. I was afraid of reading further as she accentuated that we were each responsible for our experiences by the way we think, speak and feel about things. I didn't want to be responsible for my own life; it was easier to direct everything to God. Although I was taught that God helped those who helped themselves, it was easier to remain in denial and stay ignorant. 'Let God sort it out!' I would think.

It was also easier to blame others for my frustrations, thinking they were always wrong and did things to me, and so I didn't see the speck in my own eye. If I love myself, according to the author, I would take charge of my experiences and not blame anyone for what was happening to me. I wouldn't feel sorry for myself because I was losing friends and because they had what I didn't have. I would love where I was, enjoying the moments of my freedom and finding other things to fill my life with, thus giving my own life meaning without depending on others. Well, this was certainly a mouthful and so I read further. I remained open to the knowledge, never judging nor questioning the validity of what the author was saying. I believed that she did her own research, especially on herself, when she wrote the book, knew what she was talking about, and that so far what I had read was accurate. There was no doubt that I needed to look at myself, really taking a closer look and facing up to the parts of myself that were frightened, and thus find healing.

I had two spiritual materials, a book and a magazine that would keep me busy for the entire weekend. I knew myself to be a fast reader, and didn't doubt that I would finish both the book and the magazine I had bought within two weeks, feeling optimistic that I would find some answers for the void I felt. I sensed that I was led to the finding of this book, as it revealed me to myself. I enjoyed affirmations and so affirmed every morning and evening. I read the book every day after work and completed the exercises at the end of each chapter. I began to feel myself changing and developing a positive outlook on life. I was transforming and reaching another level of my life. Completing the book took longer than I thought, as I had to stop and think with every chapter I read.

At the back of the book there was information about 'Love yourself' workshops in different countries, but I wasn't sure if they had them in South Africa. I moved over to the magazine and began paging through it casually, only reading articles that were of interest to me. On the last page of the magazine they had provided information about various workshops in every province in South Africa that focused on different spiritual subjects, and some examples of those were the self-love workshops from the book, with one being scheduled in Bloemfontein. I was thrilled to realise that I could actually attend the workshop in my own home town. Everything was coming together so well. It was then Sunday afternoon and I made a decision to call the coordinator the following day for details of the workshop.

Anneline Nel lived in De Aar, a small town almost three hundred kilometres from Bloemfontein. She was the facilitator for three provinces, including mine, and had scheduled a workshop the following month. She travelled in all three provinces arranging and facilitating these workshops. She was glad that I had called as it seemed that only a few people in my city were interested. She was so passionate about the topic that we spent at least thirty minutes on the phone. So far, only nine women had registered and so I was the tenth, and she sounded eager to meet us. She gave me details of the venue and the starting time as we said goodbye to each other and hung up. The workshop was scheduled for four and a half weeks from the time we spoke, and so I waited patiently and continued to do affirmations.

Finally, the Saturday came, and I drove to the address that Anneline had given me. It was a guesthouse, and when I went in I realised that I was not only the youngest one there but was also the only black person at the workshop. I had wondered where the men were but it didn't matter as I had found what I needed. From what I could tell, the women in the group were in their late thirties up to the age of fifty-five. I was still in my twenties.

I went directly to the lady who was busy lighting candles. I assumed that it was Anneline; all the other ladies were talking amongst themselves drinking tea. She saw me and smiled as I approached.

"Are you Kgalalelo," she said. I nodded. "I am Anneline, welcome. I'm pleased to meet you."

"Same here," I said.

"We'll be starting shortly, just waiting for two more ladies. You are twelve in the group and only ten are here, so if they don't show up in the next fifteen minutes, we'll begin. Perhaps you could help yourself to some tea in the meantime," she said. I thanked her and went to the table to make some tea and chat with the other women.

Anneline was a thin, medium-height, blonde lady, with a very high-pitched, yet calm, voice. She looked and sounded confident and one could see that the method was indeed working for her.

The remaining two ladies walked in together just minutes before we were due to start. Anneline requested all to gather around and sit on the floor. She gave each one of us a cushion to sit on. We all sat quietly and listened to her. Anneline shared the philosophy she was living by, as was the author, the theme being that if we love ourselves everything worked as we took charge of our own lives.

Taking charge of our lives meant being in control of our thoughts as our thoughts were at the root of all the problems we had in life. Listening attentively to her words, she taught us that we can reprogramme our minds and let go of the old thinking patterns. This was not an easy process since forming new thinking patterns and leaving the old behind required effort and persistence.

At the end of the workshop Anneline took us through the guided meditation process. She asked us to sit comfortably, and then guided by her voice, we were led through a series of relaxing visualisations. As we relaxed and became even more tranquil, I could feel the stress fading away and my mind becoming clearer. She had earlier explained that in meditation, when you are in this deeply relaxed state of mind, the subconscious mind was more open to positive suggestions, and therefore she gave us self-love affirmations that we repeated while in this meditative state.

I had never meditated that way before, since my form of meditation was biblical, where I was taught to read scriptures in the Bible, reflect on what I had read and then commit it to memory. Therefore Anneline's process was new to me. The two processes to my mind, however, did not differ that much since the end result was committing positive, affirming words to memory.

I continued to remain open-minded and followed Anneline's lead. There was nothing sinister about her process and therefore we willingly participated.

The workshop finally came to an end and I wondered whether I had done the process correctly, since we had visualised as directed by her words, and it was interesting to learn that way.

I continued to go to church and to enlarge my knowledge by reading other books and articles that were not necessarily Christian-based or written by Christian authors but were in line with the processes of healing the mind and with methods of changing the thinking patterns. I also familiarised myself more with the notion of meditation as illustrated by Anneline and continued with affirmations. I realised with my increasing knowledge that I had been 'thinking' all along, and my thoughts had shaped my life, but even more so my thoughts had damaged my mind.

There were many positive aspects about my life though, and I figured that that came as a result of positive thinking and trusting in God, having faith and believing that I was divinely guided every step of the way. I believed, however, that God was leading me into the inner chambers of my mind by using methods that would benefit me, root out thought patterns that were not serving me, and implant new ones; however, there had to be a process for this inner transformation and I had to be a willing participant in the makeover. This was spiritual surgery, I maintained.

I had stopped going to the bookshop for two months, ever since I had discovered 'the book', and as it was routine to go there on weekends I did again on Friday afternoon because I had left the office early. I searched the same shelf again and this time found a book about one woman's journey to physical healing, which I also bought.

The book was called 'The Journey', by Brandon Bays. Bays told an extraordinary story on how she healed a football-sized tumour by embarking on a remarkable soul-searching journey that resulted in the complete healing of the tumour. Bays contended that we can be freed from emotional baggage and physical blocks through deep transformative techniques that she described in her book.

Her philosophy was similar to the self-love approach as she

argued that the emotional baggage we were carrying around made us sick. All the negative thoughts we held about ourselves and others resulted in illnesses in the body, but if we released them then the body naturally healed itself.

It took me a week to finish reading this second book, which also offered workshops on the last page. I had nothing to lose and so called the South African number indicated to discover that the workshops this time were held in Johannesburg. One-on-one sessions were also offered and that appealed to me more. I called the facilitator, made an appointment and travelled to Johannesburg for my session.

It was easy to make an instant decision and take off at any time as I was single and didn't have any commitments. I was also fearless in trying these processes as I believed that God had brought them my way and they were indeed harmless.

I was on a journey of rediscovery and soul-searching and was willing not only to unearth as much as I could but to go through various processes that were required for my healing.

I took a six-hour bus trip to Johannesburg where I had arranged with a friend of mine who lived there to pick me up at Park Station. It was a long and tiring journey. We had to stop at a few towns for pick-up and drop-off before we reached Jo'burg.

I climbed out of the bus tired and with swollen legs to meet Lesley. I only had a handbag with me as I was to take another bus back home that evening. I didn't know the place but trusted that Lesley would take me there. I just presented him with the address and off we went. We took a taxi from the station to the residence of a man who called himself Nick.

Nick was a qualified facilitator of the 'Journey workshops' and conducted some of the personal sessions that I had come to attend. We arrived at the gate of his house and Lesley pressed the bell. We waited for a few minutes and Nick came out the door with his hands in his pockets.

"Hello there, welcome to my home," he said with a husky but

enthusiastic voice. Nick looked happy to see us. "Come on in," he said beckoning us to go inside the house.

"Oh, I won't be coming in, I only brought my friend for the session," Lesley replied.

"Okay, my name is Nick, pleased to meet you." He extended his hand to Lesley for a shake.

"I'm Lesley."

I was standing next to Lesley with a beam as the men exchanged handshakes.

He turned towards me, extended his hand and I said, "I'm Kgalalelo, good to meet you too."

Lesley then turned to look at me and asked, "What time should I pick you up, Kgali?" which is what he called me.

I was about to respond when Nick interrupted and said, "The session will take two hours at the most."

"Well, I will come later then to pick you up."

I nodded and thanked Lesley, while Nick opened the gate to let Lesley out.

I followed Nick into the house. He led me into the sitting room, which was huge and bright with white walls and cream curtains. He had a recliner in the corner of the room and a two-piece lounge suite with a beautiful wooden coffee table. I liked his house; it was airy and smelled fresh. I always loved white walls which gives the house a lovely clean look. He had two chairs next to the window and led me to one of them for the session. We sat comfortably on the chairs and Nick was all smiles. He was friendly and kind and ensured that I was really relaxed. He engaged me for about thirty minutes, needing to gather my intentions with the session and what I wished to get out of it. We talked about the book, what I liked about it and the process that he was about to follow, which was the exact same process the author followed for healing. I was open and ready, and as far as I was concerned, I was willing to try anything that promised to bring me to a state of joy and peace and a feeling of contentment in my life. Nick invited me to close my eyes and breathe deeply in and out to relax.

I had an hour and a half to go through the process and see what came out of it. It was another process of self-healing to free myself from lifetime emotional and physical blocks. The process was designed to guide me to the root causes of any ancient difficulty and then provide the tools to finally and completely resolve it. I had been taught that behind all negative emotions, difficulties and challenges there was peace that surpassed all understanding, as the Bible put it, and I wanted to plunge myself into that peace and joy.

I sank into a deep state of relaxation as I breathed in and out listening to Nick's voice as he guided me through the process. The session was almost similar to the one I had with Anneline but was more personal as I was the only one there. It seemed to be taking a long time as I was not particularly reactive to the process as he had outlined it, and when he said, "That's all for now," and I opened my eyes, I wondered if I had done the process right.

We talked for a few minutes and he said that I needed a follow-up session, but I wasn't sure if I would return as it was a long journey to get there. I then called Lesley to come and pick me up and take me to the bus station. Nick put the kettle on and prepared coffee for us. I waited for Lesley for thirty minutes and when he finally arrived, I thanked Nick for the session and the time shared together and we parted ways. Lesley and I spoke about the session on our way to the station, but I couldn't articulate in such a way that he understood what actually happened. We reached the bus station and said our goodbyes as he had another appointment. I sat at the station baffled and still wondering about my session. The bus came and I boarded and found myself a window seat.

I came home not really feeling that I had achieved my goal as described in the book, and I felt a little disappointed. I would always ask myself if I had listened carefully to the instructions and gone through the process correctly.

I continued to read anything I came across that had relevance to the teachings I was keen on learning about during that phase, and I knew I had entered another learning stage.

I was sitting in my office one day when a friend of mine, Amanda, called me one morning to let me know that she would soon be passing by my office. Her general manager had come to visit from headquarters and had scheduled a departmental session in the main boardroom. Fifteen minutes later, I heard her voice in the corridor talking to someone before she came to my office.

"Hey, listen, Vishnu is around and he is with a friend from Durban. I think he's a motivational speaker; do you want to come?" she asked.

"All right, I can really use some inspiration; let me transfer my calls quickly to the switchboard in case someone tries to reach me," I said.

We went to the boardroom and found that some of Amanda's colleagues were already there, as well as Vishnu and his friend. I was the only person from a different department who had been invited. We sat comfortably in the conference room as Vishnu welcomed everyone and introduced his friend, Jamal Naidoo.

Jamal stood and greeted everyone, before informing us that he was from the Brahma Kumaris World Spiritual University, and was in town for a few days dispensing spiritual knowledge, and that the organisation wished to open a new branch in our city. The organisation was committed to spiritual growth and personal development, and had its headquarters in Mount Abu, India.

Amanda and I looked at each other, wondering if this was a new church.

Jamal explained that the most important journey that anyone could take in their lives was the journey within. "This is the journey of who we really are and is the most important to our spiritual growth," he said, before continuing to explain that spiritual knowledge gave us the power to choose creative thinking rather than habitual thinking; that if we are spiritually mature, we respond rather than react to situations, and we experience peace instead of disorder. He paused for a moment and then continued, "Every one of us is a soul, a point of light; we therefore need to cultivate self-awareness so that we can understand ourselves."

I listened more attentively as he described the soul as having three faculties, the mind, the intellect and the personality. I was on a spiritual quest and wherever spirituality was discussed, you would find me; I suppose I attracted the events and the books. As the saying goes: 'When the student is ready, the teacher appears'.

I was interested in the science of the mind teachings, and he was elaborating even more about the faculties of the mind, where thoughts emanate. I perceived this as a further enlargement of the body of knowledge I was pursuing and that was of interest to me during that stage of my life.

By now I knew a bit more about the mind and Jamal had taken a different angle, thus building on the foundation I already had. I would say that I had begun my journey in the middle but Jamal started from the beginning by explaining who we really are. He described us as immortal souls who have taken a journey in the here and now to experience life and expand the God in us. When we die and leave our bodies, we continued to live, as a soul never dies.

Jamal continued to say that we have all been here before and we all experience a cycle of living and dying. All that we have done or did not do comes back to us. He explained that we basically reaped what we sowed, in a language I understood.

Nobody interrupted him. Everyone seemed shocked and confused and so was I. Jamal had given a lecture about karma and reincarnation and said that what happened or is happening to us was the result of causes that were set in motion in the past.

I saw a commonality in the books that I had been reading and what Jamal was saying, and that was we were each responsible for our own experiences and the choices we made in life. I found that statement bold every time I heard it, and learned that we were not victims. Although Karma and reincarnation were not biblical concepts, however, I was listening without any resistance as there was wisdom in what Jamal was teaching, and I believed that I could choose for myself that which made sense and that which didn't; that which I chose to integrate and move along with, and that which I didn't wish to carry along with me on my path. We all had the power of segregating knowledge and the key to my growth for me, I perceived, was non-judgement.

I was building up a library of books on the science of the mind teachings, and often I would pick up different and extended viewpoints and philosophies on the purpose of our incarnation, where the thought processes were of particular interest to me. I prayed prayers of protection all the time as occasionally I would feel uncertain about what I was receiving or opening myself to. I wished not to be lost in the maze. Jamal further said that we should look at the teachings about karma and reincarnation as a blessing, and pay attention, as these could help us understand why we were born with certain gifts or skills, disabilities, circumstances of our lives, our missions, and even why we were born into our own families and to the parents that we have, and that all boils down to why we are here.

The inference by Jamal met with my approval; if this could assist me in understanding the construction of life, thus removing the victim mentality that I personally had, it was something I was willing to hearken to in order to dispel uncertainies about life and questioning without proper responses. Although this was simple to grasp, however, that was not particularly the area where my interests lay.

My heart sought teachings that were geared at understanding how the mind worked, spiritually and psychologically, including techniques of healing the mind by dispelling negative thoughts forever, and was hesitant about wanting to delve into Jamal's expatiated teachings, but curiosity got the better of me. Jamal invited questions but no one raised a hand. I presumed that they were puzzled by what he had taught, since it was strange and sounded like eastern philosophy to a group of people who professed to be Christians.

In the absence of questions, Jamal invited anyone who wished to talk to him privately to do so later. I was inquisitive and wished to know more about the journey of the soul, though I felt fearful to a certain extent. I was not sure if I was treading in foreign land and could be burnt, but there was something inside me, driving me to know and to keep on digging. I felt strong and brave enough to continue my search. I kept praying and I stayed in the secret place of the Most High. God was my refuge and fortress and I trusted in Him. I believed that He wouldn't allow me to sink and meddle with things that would harm me, so I ensured that I prayed for protection and guidance all the time. If there was more to mind healing and achieving wholeness, meaning peace for twenty-four hours, I was willing to take the risk and listen with an open mind. There was surely more to what Jamal was teaching, with the exclusion of karma and reincarnation, that I believed anyone from any religious group or spiritual background could learn.

I approached Jamal whilst Amanda and her colleagues spoke to their boss.

"Hi, Jamal, I'm Kgalalelo," I said.

"Hi, how are you doing?" Jamal enquired.

"I'm doing fine, thank you, just interested in what you've been teaching," I said.

"Great! I've been wondering if I made sense and if everyone understood me. What would you like to know?" he asked.

"I'm trying to acquire as much knowledge as possible about how the mind operates, and now you have touched another topic about the soul, and I would like to know more; do you perhaps have a church where these teachings are shared?" I asked.

"We have centres all over the country, but none in Bloemfontein. I'm looking to establish one here as well. I can come to your place some time if you will allow me to and share more with you," he said.

"I would appreciate that. I live in the block of flats in the main street, in flat No. 3," I said.

"When is it suitable for me to come over?" he enquired.

"Let's make it for tomorrow after work, say about six in the evening," I answered.

"Okay, see you then," he said.

I left the conference room in high spirits, anticipating Jamal's visit so that I could learn more of what he had taught. I had moved to a new bachelor flat, with a kitchen and one huge room that served as both the bedroom and sitting room. I had a green couch for my visitors and was comfortable that Jamal should sit there while we had our conversation. At about six o'clock the following day I heard a knock on my door, and opened it to see Jamal.

"Hi, Jamal, come on in," I said.

"Hello, how are you?" he asked me.

"I'm all right; curious, but fine," I said.

"No need to worry; just relax," Jamal said giving me assurance.

Jamal had brought two huge picture frames with him and these had some information and sketches. He gave me a leaflet to browse through and said I could keep it for future reference.

Jamal began by asking me questions since he wanted to find out why I wanted to know more about spiritual matters, and especially what he had taught and the denomination I was in. I explained to him what had been going on with me, the emptiness and the subsequent journey I took. He told me I was brave as many people didn't bother much about spiritual matters, nor were they willing to listen to anything except what they knew.

He continued from where he ended during his lecture at work and gave me the opportunity to stop him whenever I needed clarification. Jamal gave me the synopsis of what he called the eternal world drama, and went on to explain the different cycles of life. I had never heard such a presentation of creation and humanity before, except what I already knew in the Bible, but the information did not differ that much, except perhaps for the terminologies.

I was a little overwhelmed by what he was teaching as some of the information seemed like a reversal of what I grew up with and taught and therefore I stopped him. We ended our session; I couldn't continue any more as I needed to interpret the knowledge on my own, and he said that I should give him a ring again if I wished to continue.

"I think that we should stop now; perhaps we can continue some other time. I need to think about what you have just said. Perhaps I should go to my prayer group leader and ask him if he knows about the teachings you offer," I said.

"Oh, sure, I would love to share this knowledge with others; just let me know when you are ready," he said.

I was confused when Jamal left but it gave me comfort to know that he would be meeting my prayer group, who perhaps would grasp it better. I went to the prayer meeting on Tuesday and told the leader about Jamal. Fortunately, he agreed that Jamal be invited to the meeting the following Tuesday and he would draw his own conclusions. I called Jamal the following day at work and he agreed to come.

The knowledge he had shared bothered me, and I tossed and turned every time I went to bed at night, and this occurred every day. I tried to make sense of it all but couldn't. I felt like he was changing my entire psychology and undoing some of the teachings I had been taught ever since I was born. Sometimes I felt as though I was going out of my mind, but at the same time I wanted to continue.

The following Tuesday Jamal came knocking on my door and we drove together to the prayer meeting. I introduced him to the group and he was given the platform. When his lecture came to an end I looked at the group leader waiting for a comment. He looked at Jamal with a smile and explained to him how he understood spirituality. He didn't want to dwell too much on what Jamal had said, and I could tell that he wasn't comfortable with the knowledge either.

Well, I had tried my best and thought that Jamal would be invited again, but that never happened. I knew that this was my road and mine alone and I had to decide what to do next.

At the flat, I synthesised everything and decided that I would never call Jamal again; perhaps I was off-track and believed things that opposed my Christian beliefs.

I wasn't eating and sleeping well, and I felt like I was going crazy most of the time. I couldn't even concentrate well at work; I thought about Jamal continually and did not have peace.

A week passed and I didn't hear anything from Jamal, but I kept wondering if I should call him. I would pick up the phone, dial his number, and then hang up before he could answer. One day, I gathered enough courage to call him, and told him I wanted to see him. I had a lot of unanswered questions and my soul was signalling for more understanding. I asked him to direct me to his house so that I could visit him there.

That afternoon, I took Amanda with me, as she lived close to his house. Jamal was a quiet-spirited person who spoke with calmness and much gentleness. He would greet you cheerfully and make you feel welcomed and accepted.

When we arrived, he met us at the gate and escorted us to the outside room of the house which he used for meditation and classes. We all removed our shoes at the door before entering the room. I liked the fact that he would explain things thoroughly to me, even such a simple thing as removing our shoes, which was for hygienic purposes, and there was nothing creepy about it.

He had invited four other people that day to share his teachings, and they joined us just before he started. He was a very time-conscious man and if he scheduled an appointment he made it on time. After the class had finished I couldn't talk to him as there were other people who wanted to engage him, and so Amanda and I left. Days passed, and I was still not settled inside. I was drawn to the teachings so much that I shocked myself. I started calling Jamal often and, this time, as my knowledge increased, I began to trust the process more and felt at ease with what I was learning. I began spending significant time with Jamal and meditating. I loved how he also explained that meditation was simply a time taken for quiet reflection and silence, away from the hustle and the activities of daily living. He was practising yet another type of meditation known as Raja Yoga meditation, which he explained was a method that didn't include rituals or chanting and which could be practiced everywhere, even with open eyes.

Jamal invited me to accompany him to one of the bigger centres in Johannesburg. We left at five o'clock on Sunday morning for a service that was due to begin at nine o'clock. He was going to introduce me to the senior sisters in the organisation. The organisation recognised the importance of women and was therefore led by women.

It was going to be the first time that I would be attending with a bigger and more well-established group which held regular sessions. I had become comfortable with him and the teachings. My consciousness was developing and I was more open to what I was hearing. Some of the questions that I had struggled with were being answered.

We arrived at the centre in Johannesburg fifteen minutes before the time. Jamal might have driven with high speed as I felt that we arrived quickly. Luckily for him there were no traffic officers on the road early in the morning.

We arrived at a double-storey house in a secluded street. There were not too many houses in that street and it was the only house that was painted white. It had a flag with the symbol of the organisation outside and when we climbed out of the car, we were greeted by people dressed in white. I took Jamal on the side to find out why everyone was wearing white, and he explained that white was a symbol of purity. Jamal was very open and approachable with me, and simplified many things for me to understand. He used pure and simple language, and there was nothing hidden in his elucidations.

I followed him into the house where we took off our shoes at the door and went to the meditation room where everyone had convened. The room was silent and only soft music was played in the background. There were no chairs and everyone was sitting on the floor. Sister Shona looked at me and nodded with a smile. I knew I was the only visitor there that morning. The smile told it all.

The atmosphere in the room was serene and everything was pure white. I loved the brightness of the room, and it calmed me down. The session started with meditation and after a while Sister Shona said, 'Om Shanti', meaning 'I am a peaceful soul', as explained to me, and the discourse began.

I came out of the room feeling refreshed and happy. It was a feeling of liberation. Breakfast was prepared for us and Jamal introduced me to Sister Shona. I will never forget how Sister Shona and everyone else made me feel that day. I felt as though I was home in my very own mother's house. There was so much love and a feeling of non-judgement. The Brahma Kumaris made me feel as if I was a part of them, and they embraced me in a way that I never knew existed. They acknowledged me and treated me as their own.

I remember how one sister made reference to the line from the movie 'Avatar' that said 'I see you'. They really recognised and accepted me. I was genuinely approved and appreciated. Brother Jamal encouraged me every time and instilled in me a feeling of fearless living, and my confidence improved. He would tell me that I was not pressured to do anything and to take my time as spirituality was in itself a journey. There was no arriving but a ceaseless process of growth, development and improvement.

More trips to Johannesburg followed after the initial one and I enjoyed going with Jamal to the sessions. I had become used to waking up early knowing that we needed to be in Johannesburg early too.

I began a long and intimate relationship with those souls. I felt at home with them, free and at peace. They considered me family and I requited and there was never a dull moment when I was with them. I was in a different phase of my life, a different season altogether. I was flourishing and enlarging in different ways and loving it.

A year and six months had passed since I had started going to the Brahma Kumaris centre for meditation. I was spending significant time with Jamal, and got to know more about the Brahma Kumaris and the work they did for the community. Jamal had mentioned that their headquarters were based in India and that members from all over the world convened there frequently for spiritual retreats, lectures and workshops.

He showed me videos he had obtained during his trips to India with the different centres and meditation halls that they had there. I welcomed what I saw; and it seemed to be a peaceful and tranquil spiritual place. I expressed my desire to Jamal to go to India, and requested that perhaps, if he went again, he would consider taking me with him. Indeed, he spoke to the elders who, surprisingly to me, agreed.

I was delighted to think that I would be going to India, which was a dream come true, and Jamal scheduled a session to take me through the preparations that I needed to make before going on the trip. One of those was to medidate every day and follow a particular diet just to ready myself. At first, I perceived this to be an easy task as I was used to praying and fasting at church, and so both sounded familiar to me. I also understood that in any organisation there are ways of doing things, there are practices to be followed and all sounded good and well. Jamal gave me time on my own to see if I could make it without his regular guidance, as at some point in time I would need to show independence and maturity.

I met up with him again a month before departure as he wanted to find out if I was ready for the trip. I had defaulted a few times with my meditation programme since I had to do things on my own. As eager as I was to go on the trip, I couldn't keep up with some of the preparatory requirements. Jamal advised that perhaps I should rather not go if I was not ready, and that the appointed time would come when I had matured and could handle responsibilities better.

He then called the elders and informed them, and they were very understanding. I was in some way disappointed that I didn't get to go to India and discover what could have happened next in my life had I travelled there.

I shifted my focus a little and tried to look for Christian texts that addressed the concept of karma and reincarnation, and a few surfaced. I searched the Internet and found some teachings by various authors. I was stunned, but knew that if I went to my prayer group with this knowledge again, I would be rebuked.

With the failure of my trip to India, I went less often for meditation classes at the centre. I decided to give myself a break and concentrate on other things.

I had acquired a vast knowledge so far in my spiritual journey from the church, with innumerable pieces of literature on the science of the mind and from the Brahma Kumaris. They all spoke about God, or a Higher Power, which was fundamental for me.

It was my intention to enhance my knowledge about God,

about who I really was as a soul, about how the mind worked and the journey of souls on earth, and the Brahma Kumaris had offered the knowledge in a way I could grasp. I had signed on for a wonderful voyage and whichever text I found opened a way for more awareness. I felt as if I was a stream flowing into the vast ocean and I allowed myself to flow.

I was spending less time with Jamal but continued to read every book he had given me to sustain myself spiritually. He had been trained to detach from anything and so he was not troubled if he did not hear from me for some time. He understood that my journey was distinct from his; he told me that he was only an instrument, conveying knowledge to those who wished to know and listen and, as the scriptures say: 'for those who have ears, let them hear.'

It was in that period that I met my soon-to-be-husband.

6

LOVE WILL FIND YOU

"Everything comes to you in the right moment. Be patient".
Eyeopenerquotes.com

I spent most of my lunch breaks alone in the office. I would close the door and read a book I had brought with me from home, and that's how I used to pass the time if I was not away on business. At other times I would visit Amanda in her office, and then we would lunch together. I still brought food I had prepared myself at home.

On one particular day I decided to take a walk to a bookshop in the nearby mall to see if I could find Christian books with topics I could be interested in. I was in the habit of buying and collecting spiritual books since I loved to read, and wouldn't think of buying any subject unless it was spiritually-related. My bookshelf was overflowing with books, some of which I hadn't read yet, but that didn't stop me from bringing a book home every now and then.

I was going through books in the Christian section when a tall and slender man walked past me. I caught him out of the corner of my eye. He stood on the other end of the shelf. I looked up and recognised him as someone I knew and had seen a few times in town. Our eyes met and with a smile he walked towards me.

"Good afternoon, lady," he said.

"Hi there, how are you?" I asked with an energetic and bubbly voice - that is who I am after all.

"I'm very well, and how are you?" he replied as he reached for a book on the shelf and then put it back and looked at me.

"I'm also fine. Are you also interested in spiritual books?" I asked.

"Yes, Christian books," he said.

"Oh, I have a lot of the Christian books at home; are you looking for anything in particular? You really look as if you are seeking something," I said.

"Actually, yes," he said.

He was looking for a book by Tim Storey, *'It's time for your comeback'*, and I had it at home. I had a collection of Christian books that I had gathered over the years. Most of the titles he mentioned, I had. We continued to talk for a few more minutes and we seemed to have a lot in common.

He was on his own spiritual journey and it was good to meet someone who was as passionate about spirituality as I was. We agreed that I would bring him the book the following day and he could come and pick it up from me at work.

"Thank you very much. I would appreciate that a lot. I can't seem to find that book anywhere, so perhaps it's out of print," he said.

"Okay, see you tomorrow; I have to rush back, my lunch-time is almost over," I said.

I left him at the book store and went back to the office.

I postponed Jamal's teachings indefinitely, and started reading Christian books again. When I got home that evening, I immediately looked for the book I had promised my new friend and put it in my handbag.

I went to work the following morning and during tea-break I received a call from the reception that someone was looking for me. I immediately presumed that it was him, took the book with me and went down to the reception to find him chatting with the receptionist.

"Hello," I said.

"Hi, good afternoon, how do you do?" he said.

"I can't complain! Well, it's good to see you again. Here's the book you wanted," I said.

"Thank you, I will bring it back as soon as I am finished," he said. He continued, "If you are not busy perhaps we could go out and discuss spirituality during lunch-time."

I didn't have a problem as I spent most of my lunch-times in the office. I thought it would be good to engage with someone at that level.

We started spending time together during lunch-time and would meet at a mutual place close to my workplace. We often got lost in conversation and so had to monitor ourselves as we both had to go back to work.

We were both really keen to talk about God whenever an opportunity availed itself - even on the telephone.

I told him about my encounter with Jamal and what he imparted to me. He would listen to me attentively and patiently and, even though we differed in some aspects, he would never criticise me but rather explained his viewpoints in a sensitive and caring way. I even told him that I was supposed to have gone to India but that the trip never materialised because I wasn't ready. I respected the fact that he didn't oppose me outright over the journey I had taken with Jamal, but would listen with an open mind to see if we could find common ground.

He was very passionate about God, and we hardly spoke about anything else except matters of the spirit. A few months passed and our friendship grew to the extent that we also started meeting during weekends to discuss matters even further. There was a non-resistant flow and communion of the spirit between us, and during that time I took a decision to go back to church, seeing that my journey with Jamal had come to an end.

I was sitting in my office on the morning of my twenty-eighth birthday when I received a call from the reception.

"Hello, who's speaking?" the voice over the phone asked.

"You are speaking to Kgalalelo, ma'm; can I help you?" I replied.

"Yes, madam, you have a delivery at reception that you need to sign for," the receptionist said.

"All right, I will be there in a few minutes."

I left my office shortly after to go to the reception to fetch my delivery. It was was a bouquet of twelve beautiful red roses. There was a card with them, but it didn't say who had sent them. I was ecstatic, signed for my delivery and went back to my office. I couldn't figure out who had sent the roses no matter how hard I thought about it. I had been receiving phone calls since I woke up in the morning from friends and family, text messages and emails, but this was even better. I rushed to the kitchen to get a vase, poured water in it and went back to the office. I was a very happy woman.

I called Amanda and my family but nobody knew about the flowers, and so I continued with my work, staring at the flowers and smiling from time to time. I felt very lucky and adored by whoever had sent them.

I received a call from my new best friend, who wished me happy birthday and asked if I had received the flowers. I was embarrassed that I had missed that as it had never occurred to me that he would be the one to send the flowers. I was totally oblivious. We made an appointment to meet after work and go out for dinner later on.

My day was filled with even more glory and text messages kept on coming through from all my acquaintances.

On that auspicious day, things began to change in my life; there was a shift that ushered in a new phase of an intimate relationship. It had never occurred to me that he looked at me in that way and, as time went on, I reciprocated.

We were at my place one Saturday afternoon and had just

finished lunch. I didn't cook very often then because I was living on my own and it was easy to prepare a quick and simple meal, but on that Saturday, because I knew he was coming, I had cooked a proper meal. As we were sitting on my green couch that I adored, he told me that he viewed our relationship seriously and that he needed to inform his pastor about me. The conversation went on for a few more minutes and I wasn't sure where it was going, but in the meantime I was thinking to myself: '*I also take this relationship seriously, but why the pastor*?" At the end of his lengthy speech, and before I could say anything, he proposed!

I looked at him with astonishment in my eyes as I tried to comprehend what had just happened. It was a marvellous surprise and I felt as though I was in a different dimension in a flash. When I came out of it, I said, "Yes, I will marry you!" I was happy and dumbfounded at the same time – and I was engaged!

There was no ring or romantic setting such as one often sees on television, but the moment was perfect - as romantic as it could get!

I had been praying for a godly partner for a while as part of my prayer points and had it on my list, but nearly missed the call by not recognising him at first. God, being the Master of everything, however, knew and always knows the byways and the highways. As He said in the Bible, "…for My thoughts are not your thoughts and My ways not your ways." (Isaiah 55:8) This occasion proved that there is perfection in existence.

The most comforting part was that there was nothing we didn't know about each other. We had had a preparatory period of a long spiritual friendship that simplified things for us. The proposal in fact came after a relatively short period of two months of dating.

We informed both our families about the engagement, and as he said he would, he informed his pastor.

I was still a member of the Pentecostal church in town, although I had defaulted in my attendance ever since I met

Jamal, and so my fiancé suggested that I join his church and let his pastor marry us. It was an easy decision to make, and I never struggled with the idea nor did I need time to think about it. I was introduced to Pastor Matthews, an elderly man of God who appeared to be the same age as my father, and his lovely wife. He held my hand and greeted me with enthusiasm and I could see fatherly love in his eyes.

Shortly thereafter I became a new member of the church and the pastor's wife took me under her wing. I had to participate in the youth activities and be part of all the other events of the church along with other congregants. We attended the youth choir practices on Saturdays in preparation for the Sunday services.

I enjoyed every bit of the time I was there, and particularly enjoyed the sermons, choruses and hymns in Sesotho, the local language in that area. I also made new friends and one of the best pieces of advice I received from Pastor Matthews when I started was that I should remove my focus on people and not put my trust in them, including himself, for my help came from the Lord, who made the heavens and the earth. He said that people could fail me, but God was faithful no matter what happened in life. That message was truly profound for me and I held on to it.

My fiancé and I attended marriage counselling sessions with the pastor, and were lovingly requested not to share anything with the congregants nor be seen together much until the pastor broke the news of the engagement to the church - just to generate excitement - and we humbly concurred. On the day that he did make the announcement I was nervous as he had called us in the day before to alert us. I knew that we were going to stand in front of the congregation so that they could all see us. I had dressed well in preparation for the occasion at least, but couldn't stop the nerves. When the announcement finally came, the whole church was excited and shouted with joy. The band went up to the stage and played heavenly music, and everyone joined in to sing praises to the Lord, while the pastor and his wife prayed for us. It was a beautiful event and we were blessed.

In the weeks to come Pastor Matthews preached about water baptism, being immersed in water in response to receiving salvation. He said it was one of the first important steps in living a Christian life. He made a call to all who hadn't been baptised and wished to be to see him after church so that he could schedule a Saturday of baptism.

I was baptised when I was an infant, and had the certificate to prove it. When the pastor explained, however, that water baptism represented inner cleansing and spiritual rebirth, I knew that there was more to it than I had thought. He went on to say that baptism gave us a new way of being and seeing things. We are raised into a new life with Christ when we are baptised, meaning that when He died we also died, when He was buried, we were also buried, and when He rose, we rose with Him too. He said with baptism every time we looked in the mirror we needed to see someone who had been raised to a new life and had a different perspective on life. I realised that what had been explained certainly meant that I had to be baptised as I now understood the meaning. What occurred when I was a baby was a symbol of baptism, but full immersion still had to occur based on the true meaning of water baptism.

I saw Pastor Matthews after the church service with other congregants and the water baptism was scheduled for the following Saturday.

About ten people showed up on that Saturday at church, the majority being young adults. The church had a pool at the back of the yard that I had never taken much notice of, and that's where all of us convened. It was summer and the weather was pleasant on that day. The pool was filled with water and after taking one look at it I felt afraid as it looked deep, but Pastor Matthews assured us that everything would be fine. He had an assistant with him, one of the elders of the church who was already inside the pool with him. He explained the process briefly to us and we lined up.

I was the fifth person in the row and I watched how the first person went in, was dipped into the water and then came out. It took only a few seconds before I gained some confidence. My turn came and I went into the pool with my hand held by the elder, and in a split second Pastor Matthews immersed me in water, and out I came! He didn't allow me to contemplate anything and start panicking but just went for it, and the process indeed took only a few seconds before it was done. I came out of the water feeling a bit disoriented and overwhelmed, but that also lasted only a moment. I had made it! I came out of the pool feeling content, and was surprised at myself that fear left me immediately when the pastor dipped me. I grabbed my towel and went to the ladies' room to change. I walked tall and couldn't wait to share the news with my fiancé.

I had been a single woman for a while, trying to find myself and understand what I wanted in life, and my journey of self-discovery had led me into an exciting spiritual path that opened me up and taught me countless things. I made friends along the way who supported me without reservation and who were going through the same growth process that I was. I didn't know what I would find; life was just a huge surprise. I had surrendered any expectation of how things would show up in my life and floated with the current. I immersed myself in spiritual books daily to keep my sanity and enlarged my consciousness even more. Spending time with God and being positive were the only things that made sense and carried me to safety.

While reminiscing about the baptism that evening and feeling like a new person, my thoughts flashed back to the entire journey that had brought me to where I was that day. I remembered sitting at the salon doing my hair on one occasion; I had parked my car outside the hairdresser's house and I could see it when she said, "You know, Kgalalelo, independent women like yourself never get married and never find life partners. Men are afraid of women who have cars and houses; you are too independent." I loved my hairdresser, she understood my needs, and because of the soft texture of my hair, she always handled it with care. I had been going to her hair salon for some time. I knew that she would be the one to style my hair for the wedding and so I laughed. Her words didn't shock me at all; what she said was common.

I know many people say so in magazines, on television, radio and via other channels. Those who had successful careers, with cars and houses, were ruled out of marriage, and whether this was true or not, to me it was a matter of the mind and what people individually believed. I was loaded with knowledge and experience and nothing could keep me from enjoying my life to the full. I read a book by Susan Wales that I had bought from the bookstore called 'Standing on the Promises'. Wales said that single women ought not to put their lives on hold whilst waiting for life partners. She stated that they should carry on living their lives with grace, and at the right time God would provide the perfect match for a partner. It was important that those desiring partners should put their complete trust in the Lord and have faith that what they prayed for would come to pass. I therefore believed her words of encouragement and moved on with my life. Only God knew the perfect mate and the perfect timing for provision.

My life was lived through prayer, and even the encounter with my future husband was no accident. I learnt from experience that God had infinite resources of provision and He hardly used our own approach. His methods always said 'Amen' in the spirit of the one who asked. He knew how to mix and match based on His divine purpose for our lives. My husband later told me that he had also been praying for the right partner, and our meeting was a divine happening. I possessed all the qualities he had desired in a mate, and so did he for my desires.

What followed were the preparations for our wedding, and even those we put before God in order to be exactly what we desired. We relied on the scripture that said: "Delight yourself in the Lord and he will give you the desires of your heart." (Psalm 37:4) This scripture was perfect for the kind of wedding we were dreaming and speaking about.

It was my desire to have my wedding in the city I was living in so that I could plan it myself, and, besides, most of my friends and colleagues were also living in the city. I presented the proposal to my parents, and the reasons, and they never objected. They accepted my plans and desires and gave me their utmost support. There was also no indication that any of my relatives were opposed to the proposal. That was the first piece of the puzzle that amazed me.

It is the black South African tradition for the bride to prepare herself at her parents' home and be escorted to the wedding ceremony from her parents' house, but I had a home of my own, and it was easier for me to dress from my own house, which my parents understood without reservation.

My husband's family lived fifty kilometres from the city and the church was also in the same area. The venues that we chose for the wedding ceremony and the reception were both in town, and even this we placed before the family and the church leadership, who agreed that we could have everything in the same locale. The church had never had any wedding ceremony outside the premises and so this was a first in the history of the church. The only requirement from the elders was that we choose bridesmaids and groomsmen in the church, which was our plan in the first place and was gratifying as we were part of the youth ministry. So our desires were in harmony, and only God could arrange it this way. He was remarkable with everything down to even the smallest detail.

My fiancé and I continued to pray for our wedding, and we

even asked God for perfect weather conditions on the day of the wedding - and that's what we got, a bright, 'sunshiny' day. Everything was easy and effortless, and whatever we touched turned to gold. Finances were extraordinarily available to enable us to pay for everything and some of the things were even done for us by other people without payment. My friend from Pretoria offered to make the invitation cards free of charge, and I only had to purchase the material she intended using. Another friend offered to 'deejay' at the wedding without charge, and even brought his own equipment and music.

In addition to her catering skills, the caterer was also a florist, and the entire décor was left to her - needless to say, she did an incredible job. I saw the venue transformed into an awesome white and gold pattern that I once dreamed of.

My wedding day became a point of reference for everything I wanted to achieve afterwards. I had seen the hand of God in my life before; when I looked back, I could see that He had always been with me and nothing was a coincidence in my life; our move from Vaal Reefs to Mafikeng had shaped me to a certain level, and other events that followed made me realise that I had been in God's palm all of my life. I might not have noticed the many times that God saved me, but, as I grew older and saw many more concurrences, I became aware of His hand in my life. All challenges I had faced made me a stronger person and brought me closer to God. There were never hiccups with the preparations for the wedding.

My husband and I were married in December of 2005 in an amazing ceremony in front of two hundred people comprising friends, family and the church. It was one of the best days of my life. The wedding was followed by the traditional welcoming of the bride ceremony the following day at my husband's home. My uncles and aunts escorted me and presented me to the family. We stayed with my husband's family only for a night, and the following day we left as we already had our own home and our own plans. I was well received by my in-laws and wondered why some of my friends complained about theirs. Perhaps it was just a bad habit that they'd picked up from their own friends in believing that the in-laws, especially the mother-in-law, have to give the newlyweds a hard time. It was not like that with me.

We left the following day after lunch to go to our own home, waving goodbye to the family, and spent the rest of the month revelling in marital bliss.

I went back to work during the second week of January 2006. I was happy, grateful and peaceful. Nothing could disturb the peace and joy I was feeling. As I entered the building, I met one of the cleaning ladies, an elderly woman in her sixties. She looked at me and saw the ring on my finger.

"Hello, my child, I haven't seen you in a long while; did you get married over the holidays?" she asked, holding my hand. "Your ring looks beautiful."

I was blushing as she was talking, and then I said, "Thank you, *Mama*; I did get married in December."

With a rather jolly face, she asked, "Why did you get married, my child, when marriage is so full of misery?"

I didn't know what to say to her. She smiled again and walked away. I went into the elevator wondering why she had said all that she did say, and I felt a bit agitated. Mama Dixie was a nice, matured woman, but I was really disturbed by what she had said. I was a newly-wed, only three weeks married, and all I expected to hear from colleagues were congratulatory messages, and nothing discouraging. I thought about her statement all the way to my office and, as I was thinking about her words, the thought came to my mind that this woman might have had a really tough marriage, and I decided to ignore her statement.

I remembered Denise and her husband. They loved each other and the picture of their marriage that I saw was nothing like what the old lady had described. Pastor Matthews and his wife showed me another picture of marriage that I appreciated.

The pastor was affectionate to his wife in church and treated her with respect. I didn't know what the old lady was talking about and, with that, I decided to lay these fears to rest and not assimilate them. It's amazing what effect the words of other people can have in our lives, but it is really up to us whether we choose to believe what they say, or to hold on to another image of what we desire to see. I saw that while I was growing up, with all that was hurled at me, people might say that this was a cliché, but we really do have a choice as to what goes on in our minds. It becomes easier, though, when you are mature, especially spiritually. As a child, you would feel lost most of the time, until you finally find the grip of who you really are.

I had seen my parents and many relatives living together in their marriages and pulling through all the time, and Denise had once told me that one day when I get married, God would enable my husband and me to sail through the storms of life together and come out victorious, and I believed her. I chose to absorb her words and imprint them in my mind.

I would describe the first year of our marriage as undeniably wonderful, unlike what Mama Dixie had thought it would be. My husband and I had infrequent arguments, but nothing we couldn't resolve, and it was humbling to me that I had found someone who was supportive and understanding. I fell pregnant in the very same year, effortlessly, and the pregnancy was easy to carry. I thanked the Lord that once again He had given us grace. There are many couples who try to conceive after marriage and struggle, and to me it was a natural occurrence. I discovered that I was pregnant within eight weeks of conception and every visit to the gynaecologist was a success. The baby was growing remarkably well and enjoyed its time in my womb. The joyful kicks confirmed it.

We were blessed with a beautiful, healthy, bouncy baby girl in 2007, and she became the joy of our lives. I spent the first two weeks after giving birth with my mother in Klerksdorp as she needed to teach me how to take care of the baby, and then I went back to Bloemfontein. It was not easy without my mom by my side during the first few months, but my husband was there to help me. I had to learn how to bathe that tiny little one, and the sleepless nights were many. I presumed that everyone goes through that stage when they have babies.

The second year was hectic with the baby around the house. All the attention was centred on her. I had spent five of my six months maternity leave with her at home, although it was not an easy task to manage, before we looked for a nanny.

My husband and I would have differences of opinion on how to take care of the baby. As a mother, I thought it was my place to decide on everything, I thought I had the so-called natural instincts, but I learnt a thing or two from my husband. Admission, well, was not my strongest point.

Likewise, living together was not the easiest thing to do as time went on. It had its own trials, or rather I observed myself negating some of my husband's sentiments and he would some-times deny mine.

Perhaps it took us to the concept of 'the honeymoon being over'. My husband had his own vision of things and I had mine. The only way, however, that we could come to agreement about things was by means of constant communication. At times, I would feel that communication was not working for me, as it led to more disputes, but in the end, there was always a solution and the soil smelled nicer after the rain.

We realised on our own that, in the midst of constant commu-nication, we should love and respect each other and choose words carefully, as whatever had been said could not be reversed. This, of course, took time for us to understand. We essentially learnt through trial and error but, as they say, love conquers all. I real-ised that marriage is a constant practice of weeding and pruning dead leaves in yourself, and to see changes, you had to change your perception about one another and exercise a great deal of patience. Being spiritually inclined made us look at each other as souls and children of God, and this made the load lighter.

Mama Dixie's assumptions were still false. Perhaps that is what she meant about the challenges of marriage, but her expression portrayed fear more than anything else. I concluded that marriage was a spiritual journey on its own that could only be managed with the grace of God, for the Bible says: "My grace is sufficient for you, for my power is made perfect in weakness." (2 Corinthians 12:9)

We continued to go to church every Sunday as we normally did, but I decided to revisit the new thought literature that I still had on my bookshelves. I believed that every path that I had taken in my life had brought me to the light. All the knowledge I had obtained made me know God even better, and there was truth, my truth, in what I had learnt. I appreciated the new thought teachings I had acquired, the people I had interacted with in my spiritual journey and the countless books I had read. All had contributed to making me the person I was, and denying them was the denial of myself. The power of positive thinking, other mind healing practices, affirmations and open eye meditation were some of the techniques that resonated with me more in my overall spiritual pack.

Jamal had always taught me that one needed to hold a meditative state while being engaged in everyday life, as in cooking, driving, working, in other words attunement with God in every waking moment, hence meditating with open eyes. That was still relevant. I wanted to revisit and explore his teachings more on understanding the 'self', and how to purify the thoughts, as I knew that our thoughts guided us to our destinities and the reality we wanted to create. It was not that I was not hearing some of the similar teachings during Sunday church services, but the expression and expatiation from various authors and teachers assisted me in comprehension. The method of teaching and practice of the fields of knowledge also differed in particular ways.

Moreover, I realised that I also appreciated being taught in a classroom setting where I was given an opportunity to engage, receive clarity and apply the knowledge in class and with one-on-one sessions and processes.

The methods therefore, harmonised with the process of education I was similarly preferring.

I was hesitant to inform my husband for fear that he would have the perception that I intended leaving the church, which was not the case. All I required was to enhance my spiritual knowledge using other practices in the sea of knowledge that already existed, and specific subjects appealed to me and strengthened what I had already received.

I prayed about the matter and presented it to God, who already knew in any case the issues of my heart. I needed wisdom in approaching this with the correct words that would not be misinterpreted in any way. This was a matter of my awareness increasing and being hungry to understand better.

My husband came home one day with the DVD of 'The Secret' by Rhonda Byrne, and asked me to watch it with him. His supervisor had lent it to him, along with the audiobook. He had listened to the audio during lunch break at work and thought it could be something that might intrigue me. I had heard a little about 'The Secret' but never paid much attention. The title didn't sound attractive to me.

I agreed to watch it nevertheless, and became remarkably glued to the screen within a few minutes of starting to view. I was inspired and didn't want any interruption as I listened to what the different speakers in the film were articulating. I instantly experienced a connection to my soul. There was an activation in my spirit that made me realise how blessed I was, and how much I was surrounded by love, friendship, abundance and kindness. The attributes verbalised were common to what I had gathered all these years, but I just wasn't familiar with the concept of the law of attraction in my walk to describe what I had assimilated. I recalled and recognised how everything synchronised in my life that brought me things I had sought after. I had been led to workshops one after another, books, great teachers, websites and organisations that all contributed to a fount of knowledge that advanced me. I knew that God had brought everything to me because I was properly aligned to what I desired. Attunement was the single word I could come up with to describe this magnificence.

I was startled that my husband had taken an interest in the law of attraction. He even introduced me to similar books in the same genre. We discussed the law of attraction frequently. I had tried to share some of the concepts with him using different terminology, but we couldn't reach consensus. Now that he was the one who introduced me to the law of attraction, I could easily communicate some of the new thought principles I was accustomed to without fear of condemnation.

I bought the book and spent days and nights reading and absorbing the material.

I valued the practice of gratitude and understood perfectly how gratitude diminished negative thinking, and I decided to make it a part of my daily life. I started a gratitude journal and conversed with God differently, acknowledging every day the blessings I had in my life and being grateful in advance for all other things I wished to experience. I wrote a minimum of a hundred things I was grateful for daily and kept my journal in my handbag. I carried it with me wherever I went and as my awareness of the grace of God increased, I would take the journal out and record my feelings. It mattered not where I was, my gratitude journal was my new best friend and I would pull it out wherever I was and whenever I deemed it necessary to document my day as I went along.

Prayer also began to have a new meaning in my life, so instead of lamenting to God about a few things that were going wrong, I expressed gratitude for the many things that were going right.

I left my prayer sessions feeling good and peaceful.

The practice of the knowledge of the law of attraction affected all areas of my life. My work activities for as long as I was aligned and practising gratitude were easy and effortless, my relationships with people all around were wonderful, and I prospered in all the things that I did. I was joyful all the time and loved how I felt. My body was light and I relished perfect divine health. It was a working formula for me. I related better to my husband because my attitude improved and I would remember to mention him when giving gratitude, either through vocalised prayer or written prayers in my journal. Revisiting my entries ensured that I remembered every aspect of life as well, since one occasionally became entangled in the drama of life.

7

PUSHING THROUGH

"Even though I walk through the darkest valley, I will fear no evil, for you are with me; your rod and your staff, they comfort me."
Psalm 24:4

I have always had a probing mind when it comes to matters of spirituality and an open mind when listening to different perspectives. I prayed for protection and clarity every time I went to a spiritual session of interest and invited God's covering. I carried on with the practice of gratitude and journaling and never missed a day. As my awareness increased I began attracting to myself other spiritual subjects that were not necessarily within the scope of how I was learning.

I came home exhausted from work one afternoon and plunged on to the couch for a little while before preparing supper. I switched on the television and started flipping channels. I came across a talk show that was on and captured a discussion on hypnotherapy. I never watched television very much as I preferred to indulge in books, and as a result did not even obtain the name of the show.

I stood up and went to the kitchen but the key word was impressed on my mind. I had requested two days leave from work to rejuvenate and spend time in God's presence. I had been feeling consumed by innumerable work responsibilities and was depleted. I determined to visit the bookstore the following day and research the topic I had picked up on television.

I started at the gym for my exercise routine in the morning, went for a ten-minute sauna and took a shower. I got into the car and went to the mall afterward, and the bookshop was the last place on my mind. I needed a few items for the home first and so moved around. There was nothing to beat a hot cup of coffee at the mall and so I walked to a restaurant and treated myself to a full breakfast. My husband was at work and I had the whole day to myself.

I remembered that I needed to go to the bookstore and so left when I had paid for the breakfast. The bookshop was situated on the second floor and I took the escalator that led me right into it. I went directly to the mind, body and spirit section, and started searching for no particular book, but any book that addressed hypnotherapy. They had a psychology bookshelf next to where I was standing and I explored that too.

I came across some interesting titles on the brain and perception, hypnosis, how to use the subconscious mind, and a few on past-life therapy. Past-life therapy was not a new concept to me as it was integrated in the teachings of karma and reincarnation I had learnt about from Jamal.

I discovered that hypnotherapy was "a form of psychotherapy used to create subconscious change in a patient in the form of new responses, thoughts, attitudes, behaviours or feelings". The participants are usually put under hypnosis. ('Hypnotherapy' from Wikipedia)

One the other hand, Dr Hilary Jones (1988) states that "Hypnotherapy aims to re-programme patterns of behaviour within the mind, enabling irrational fears, phobias, negative thoughts and suppressed emotions to be overcome." Hypnotherapy thus promotes healing and helps with a positive mindset.

I came to learn that the idea of hypnotherapy was simply

geared at helping people make positive changes in themselves and through the process, although people are in fact in control of what is happening and can stop the session at any time. This idea of hypnotherapy as far as I was concerned was parallel to guided meditation that I had gone through with different spiritual teachers, including Jamal. The procedure was the same and the teachers or therapists were basically facilitators of the process that I was in control of.

As I was going through the shelves, I came across a book by Brian L. Weiss, M.D., titled: 'Many Lives, Many Masters'. I pulled it out, found a seat in the aisle and paged through. Weiss is both a psychiatrist and hypnotherapist who focuses on past life regression, including reincarnation.

I took the book with me to the counter, paid for it and went home. I was still on vacation leave and was not in a hurry to read it, and so I placed it in my bookshelf.

When the two days were over and it was time to return to work, I woke up at 5:30 on the first day, went to the bathroom, took a bath, and thanked God for a fruitful and successful day. I left early, as I wanted to pray at the office as well before everyone arrived. It was a short commute to the office and, as expected, nobody was there except the security officer at the door. On seeing me he opened the door and greeted me and I proceeded via the elevator to the third floor, where my office was.

A few minutes later I took the book out of my handbag and went through it. I had only thirty minutes to myself before everyone started arriving.

As I began my day's work, I placed the book on the desk, hoping to get a few minutes during tea break and even lunchtime to continue. Just then Ann, a colleague of mine, entered my office to give me a report about the progress of her son, who had fallen ill.

When her eyes fell on the book she said, "Wow, Kgalalelo, what is this book you are reading? What is it all about?" She picked it up from the table, read the title and then opened it. I explained to Ann that there is evidence in that book and others that we have lived before, and that this data could be accessed through hypnosis and other means. Many people have been regressed and have experienced their past lives. Some of the illnesses and blockages in our lives have been attributed to events that occurred in our past lives, and as we reincarnated we still experienced similar resistance and pain.

I explained the concept of reincarnation to her, as she wanted to know more, but was careful not to cloud her judgement. Ann was not concerned, but excited, and we talked more.

"You know, I always felt that when I die I will observe and experience my burial," she disclosed.

I was taken aback about her interest in this and wondered how many people knew about reincarnation in the society I lived in, but were too anxious to come out for fear of reproach. Reincarnation was an unheard-of word to many people I knew, and in the black community the locals were predominantly Christians.

We ended our conversation and when she asked to borrow the book as soon as I had finished I nodded.

I had to leave the office shortly after as I had to meet with the manager of human resources. On my way there, I made a detour to the office of Dorothy in the workforce planning division. I was friendly with everyone in the building and people knew me.

Dorothy had just joined the organisation a few months back, a beautiful and charming lady who always attracted the attention of the males in the building. She was tall and slender with a huge afro hair style. I often told her to find a modelling agency as I thought she met the height and stature requirements of models. I saw her on the runway in my imagination.

Dorothy was on the phone and so I entered as the door was open. There was a book lying on top of her table as well; I picked it up, made myself comfortable on the chair and searched the pages while she was still busy. I was surprised to see the book featuring spiritual laws, with karma and reincarnation amongst them.

'Why would such a classy lady be reading about spiritual laws?' I thought in ignorance.

I waited for her to finish her conversation on the phone and when she hung up she said with a beautiful smile, "Hi there, how have you been?"

"Hi, Dorothy, I should ask you the same. I haven't seen you in a while," I replied. "But what is this book you are reading? What do you know about karma and reincarnation?" I probed, as I was astonished.

She gave a loud and hearty laugh.

I had never spoken to nor asked anyone about these ideas, and realised that the lack of dialogue didn't mean that nobody knew anything. I gathered that some people in the society were opening up to the ideas and knew something about them. It was coincidental that I had met two people at work on the same day who happened to be curious about reincarnation as I was. The events just connected and I considered that I must have been led to them, and I might have attracted the dialogue.

"I am as curious as yourself, Kgali," she said to me. "I have had my fair share of life's experiences that made me start searching for meaning. I am on a journey of self-discovery and I bumped into that book."

"I am stunned!" I said as I put the book down.

"I am meeting a hypnotherapist for a past life regression session later today," Dorothy uttered.

"Are you sincere?" I asked with wonder. "Are you seriously going to have a session, Dorothy, or are you teasing?"

I was intrigued and asked for the hypnotherapist's number. I thought, *'This is it; I will finally get all of the answers about my journey on earth.'*

I believed that I would be able to discover the reasons for my journey in this incarnation, the spiritual reasons for our move from one place to the other, all the experiences I had as a child and as an adult, and the challenges that I faced sporadically. I thought about this in linear terms and this session seemed like the solution to my problems in order to fill the gaps. I thought about the liberation I would experience and joy filled my soul.

I left Dorothy's office in a good, soulful space, went to the meeting at human resources and then returned to my office. I carried the joy in my heart as I worked, and every activity was light and effortless. I wanted to make an appointment with the hypnotherapist for my session and towards the end of the business day I dialled her number.

"Yes, who is this?" I heard a warm and kind voice on the phone.

Debra Jones was a Britisher. Her family had moved from Scotland in the 1900s and had relocated to Johannesburg, where she grew up. Her father had been a businessman while her mother stayed at home to raise her and her siblings. As a child, she was captivated by pottery and took classes as she grew up, nursing a passion that later developed into a means of living. She met her husband Gerrie, an Afrikaner man, at one of the expositions of her pottery and other artwork. She worked from home after the birth of her two sons, and often spent many days alone with the kids when Gerrie was away travelling.

She found her love for spirituality when she was invited by a friend to a meditation class and since then had attended courses to enhance her knowledge and qualify herself as a hypnotherapist.

Debra could see me the next day at 15h00, and so we scheduled an appointment.

As I hung up the phone, my mind ran wild as I imagined knowing about my past lives and how I related to everyone who was currently in my life.

I left the office shortly after to go home, and informed my husband about the session. I prayed about the matter that night before going to sleep and invited God to go before me to the session, asking for His protection. I wasn't sure what to expect since this was my first experience, but I was open to the idea and trusted that if anything went amiss, God would direct me.

The following morning I went to work as usual, but my mind was on the afternoon session awaiting me. I thought about what it would be like to know about how I had lived before, what I did and how had everything affected me in my current life. Most of all, I thought about what would happen next as soon as I discovered my past lives. The anxiety grew as the hours went by, but I was still keen on going. I left the office twenty minutes before the appointment as Debra lived just three kilometres from my workplace. I avoided disturbances of any kind the whole day especially from people, as my focus was on the session.

At 14h30 I started clearing my table, and switched off my computer. I then took my handbag and headed to the car park outside. I was not in a hurry as it was only a few minutes drive to get there, and so I drove very slowly. It still took me only five minutes, since there was no traffic and the robots were kind. I parked the car on her driveway and sat in the car for a few minutes as it was still early. I assumed that she might have been in another session with a client and wished not to disturb them. I took out a book from my handbag and kept myself busy until it was time to go in. I knocked on the front door and a huge man opened the door, someone I assumed had to be Gerrie.

I greeted him and asked if Debra was in, but was told that she had gone quickly to the bank and would be home soon. Gerrie offered me a chair on the veranda and I waited. I was comfortable sitting outside as it gave me a chance to look around. The anticipation was killing me, and I kept on looking at my wristwatch. It was almost three o'clock when I heard the sound of a car in the driveway; the engine died and the door opened. A middle-aged woman climbed out of the car and walked towards me. I had had funny ideas about how she would be dressed, bohemian-like, but she had normal clothing on, short denim pants and a brown T-shirt. I recognised though that she had a small tattoo of a rose on her left toe. Her smile was pretty and her voice precisely as I had heard it on the phone. I was thrilled when I saw her as the moment had come and she was finally there. She welcomed me by extending her hand for a shake, and invited me into the house. We entered a spacious living room with brilliant white walls, and the beige curtains hung neatly on the windows. The furnishings were mostly brown with a tinge of beige to match the curtains. I noticed a large portrait of pottery pots on the wall with rich red and orange colours. It was a beautiful room to observe. On the left side of the room was an archway that led to the kitchen. I caught a glimpse of the clean carpentry finish of the cupboards. I followed her across the room and we came to a closed wooden door that she opened, and we went in.

We had entered her consultation room. Soft meditative music was playing gently and I could smell the woody and sweet scent of sandalwood incense. It took me back to the times when I was still attending Mass at the Anglican Church.

Debra later told me that sandalwood was one of the most calming incenses, and was one of those preferred for meditation. It calmed the mind and enhanced mental clarity. Incense was used for different religious rites, and at Mass I learnt that the incensing and the symbolic value of the smoke purified and sanctified the area. The smoke also symbolised the prayers of the faithful drifting up to heaven.

The room was furnished with comfortable and beautiful brown couches with frilled auburn scatter cushions on top. The brown colour with the deep red undertone seemed to be Debra's colours, I noticed. They were the colours of mother earth. Debra had a gigantic bookshelf at the far end of the room against the wall and a large massage table that she used for Reiki energy healing.

I knew about Reiki from Jamal and had a session with one of the sisters at the centre when I was still attending meditation classes with him.

Reiki is one of the most widely known and used healing techniques from the Japanese for stress reduction and relaxation. It is based on the belief in the existence of one universal energy of God. Using this technique, practitioners believe that they transfer healing energy through their hands. The healer thus lay hands on the recipient to convey universal life energy to the area of the body that needs healing (The International Center for Reiki Training, 1990-2016).

The laying on of hands is and has been a practice in Christianity for ages and is similarly used for healing purposes. That was a topic for another day and another time, for my interest at that moment was on past life regression.

The room had an altar next to the window for natural light and there were sacred ornaments on top; angel candleholders and a wooden cross.

Debra showed me to a chair and handed me a form to complete that contained contact details, nature of the visit and comments. It took me a few minutes to complete and then we began the session. She conducted a short interview to get to know me better, and explained how she became a hypnotherapist and the work she was doing. She was well-established from what I gathered and saw clients on a weekly basis. She had a full schedule and I was fortunate to get an earlier appointment as someone had cancelled. We spoke about the regression and what I hoped to gain from it. She had sessions herself with another therapist and the more she gave information about her credentials, the more relaxed I became. She prayed before beginning hypnosis and coached me to be comfortable, with my eyes closed, and to relax.

I listened to the soft guidance of her voice and the low sound of meditative music in the background as I went into a deep state of relaxation. The process was similar to Anneline and Nick's guided meditation routines we had performed some time back, and was not strange at all. While I was in meditation she engaged me with suggestions and questions to help remove blockages and unravel the mind. I observed that my mind wandered and I would try to bring it back to her voice, manage that for a minute, and then lose focus again. She carried on for thirty minutes, which felt like an hour as I grew in frustration. When the allocated time of the session ended I knew that I did not achieve the goal. Debra had conducted the process the best way she knew how as far as her training as a hypnotherapist was concerned, but I did not respond well to the therapy again.

I realised that, as much as I wanted to know it all, prayed about it and claimed to have surrendered, I never completely let go. I held back and resisted. I wasn't allowing myself to go deep into the subconscious mind; the conscious mind was active throughout the session and reasoning.

I drove home after the session disappointed and on arrival I went into the bedroom thinking about what had happened. I was discontented and argued with myself that perhaps the process was not for me; I was not meant to meddle with things like that, but on the other hand I contended that it was a scientific procedure used by psychologists and therefore it was not harmful. Maybe every therapist did it differently, but I viewed it the same nevertheless. Whether using it for past live regression or regression to the point of birth or childhood, it all seemed the same to me, and I achieved none of that.

I picked up my book about past lives later that day, but the fire that was there before about this knowledge was not there any more. I felt discouraged as I was enthusiastic about the procedure, and thought I had failed. I had believed that God would help me remember something about my past, but I gained nothing from the session. I was not concerned much about the money I had paid but more that the session didn't yield any results: not because the therapist failed but because I hesitated. I had seen God perform miracles in my life, guiding me and providing me with the things I had asked for. I had asked for this as well but it didn't bear any fruit. I had even believed that my chance meeting with Dorothy was divinely ordained and I was meant to go for the therapy, but was not so sure any more.

"Perhaps I wanted to put God in a box and assumed that was part of His will for my life," I thought to myself.

I came up with all sorts of reasoning that should make me feel better, but nothing worked.

I had pictured myself calling my cousin Given, Martha and Amanda and telling them who I was in the previous life, what I had done wrong and what I was here to correct, if there was something to correct. Given and Jamal had advised me not to tamper with what had passed and just concern myself with my present incarnation, but I was stubborn.

Exhaustion consumed me and my entire body was worn out, so I went to bed early that day. I carried the fatigue through to the next day, but had to go to work. I dragged myself out of bed in the morning, took a quick shower and dressed. I skipped breakfast as my appetite had gone, and drove off to work.

It was a long journey to work as I drove the slowest I had ever done that day. All other cars had to pass me as I put my car into a lower gear. My mind was reeling and my eyes heavy. I stopped at the robots and closed my eyes for a moment; the cars hooted behind me as the robots had turned green and I had nearly dosed off.

My concentration level was poor the entire day and I needed to sleep. I took a nap during lunch-time and half an hour before knock-off time I asked my supervisor to release me. The tired-ness became worse the moment I entered my yard. I felt it from my back to the chest, and I suffered from a shortness of breath.

Later on as I tried to de-stress, my legs felt heavy too and on fire, hot from the inside, but when I touched them they were the normal temperature.

My two-year-old daughter came rushing in and touched them too as she saw me doing it, and I convinced myself that there was healing energy in her hands. I didn't feel any different, though, and I remembered that I had a vibrating foot spa massager that I could use; I got hold of it, poured warm water in, plugged it in and dipped in my legs. The tension subsided.

My husband came home later that evening with a local newspaper that I took from him. As I paged through I came across an interview with a former drug addict who shared her story about how she overcame drugs. The woman said that, like many other addicts, she tried countless times to break off the habit but failed at every attempt. She said she met a friend who told her that God could help her and that He was willing and able to set her free from the power of drugs. She said the moment she surrendered everything to God and believed that God was her only hope for transforming her into a better being, things began to change. She was surrounded by people who encouraged her and prayed for her. She let go and continued in prayer, and the craving for drugs disappeared. I read with much interest because I knew the power of God in my life. I had one testimony after the other about how He walked with me and guided me in every phase of my life. Most of all, He protected me no matter what activity I engaged in. I knew that the grace of God was upon me and whether the session felt wrong or right, it was all good. There was a reason for it going that way, and I needed to relax and not to worry. I felt the discouragement lift at just reading that story and I resolved to pay attention and trust the process of life. God surely knew what He was doing. I closed the newspaper and dozed off. Mission accomplished!

I felt energised the following day and went to Dorothy's office as I was curious about how her session turned out. She had decided to cancel the appointment as she was not very keen any more about the approach.

8

CLEARING THE CONFUSION

"I am the Ocean of Love; I show you the depth of love.
My love remains unbroken and constant.
I have so much love for you, and My love is
unconditional and unlimited.
I am the Beloved. You have been calling out to Me for a long time."
Brahma Kumaris World Spiritual University

My quest for the truth increased by the day, but I couldn't rest with the knowledge I had acquired and claim that I had arrived. I would flip channels on television on Sundays as they had a range of spiritual programmes, and viewed them for the better part of the day. Many spiritual seekers in various religious organisations proclaimed the wonderful doings of God, calling Him by different names. I would stand up, sing and dance to the gospel music shows and connect with God and go to another channel to find souls in meditation with soft, tranquilizing music, and feel still closer to God.

I remember watching one of these programmes in which the television presenter had visited the home of a holy man who kept on referring to God as 'the Beloved', and that sounded so good to me as the word just warmed my heart. Issues relating to faith were discussed, and everyone spoke passionately about their faith, but one thing they all had in common was that they believed in the one and only God in Heaven who was within all of us. I would sit there listening until the programme came to an end, then find a quiet place to reflect. I thought deeply about spiritual matters and at times would wonder if my husband thought I was crazy to tackle so many aspects.

I was led into the expansion that unfolded every day as I would think that I had found the 'real thing' but that 'real thing' would lead me to another one, and then another, and I would find myself in the deep end of the unending pool of spiritual knowledge. My family knew that I was in a church and that I was learning through Jamal too, and that I would share knowledge with them and introduce them to some of the concepts that I thought were easy for them to comprehend. I saw similarities all the time and it was a matter of phraseology while spiritual disciplines all referred to the same thing. I could never put God in a box or contain Him. He was and still is vast.

The scripture that says, "For all things are possible with God," (Mark 10:27) was real and the total truth for me.

I also grew up with a Setswana hymn that goes:

'Bogolo jwa Bomodimo, bo ka angwa ke Mang?'
(*Who can fathom the greatness of God?*)

'Oa ikapesa ka maru,'
(*He clothes Himself with the clouds*)

'O palama phefo,'
(*He rides the winds*).

Those words sank deep into my mind and I always stood in awe when I sang that hymn. I knew it by heart from singing at school during the morning assembly and sometimes in church and never sang from the hymn book. Given and Martha were the two people whom I spoke to most of the time about my experiences as they understood me better. My husband was wonderful and supportive and never really judged me. He would engage me and ask questions as he felt that it was his responsibility as my partner to look after me and ensure that I wasn't derailed, and end up doing things that could harm me. I was grateful that he involved himself also in my quest. He had his own moments of bewilderment about spirituality and was on his own journey. When things challenge you in life and at times tough times arise, you would question and wonder if God was with you. Therefore he understood that I was finding myself and this seemed like a lifetime mission. His support meant the world to me and he would often say that Jesus said, "For whoever is not against us is for us." (Mark 9:40)

The scripture encouraged me as I knew I was not lost - I might have been in a maze but I was definitely not lost. I was on a path I thoroughly enjoyed and walked with confidence and pleasure. I found that there was delicate resonance everywhere I was seeking and the more I sought the more I found.

I was unlocking the mysteries of God and with the passage of time I accidently stumbled across the title of a book by Elizabeth Clare Prophet called 'Access the Power of Your Higher Self' on the Internet. There was a brief synopsis of what the book was about and I looked for purchasing details. I could buy it online from the USA, but the shipping would take two weeks. I sent an e-mail to the address allocated to find out if I could get it in some other way, and was given the contact details of someone in Pretoria who had the book. I spoke to the man on the phone, ordered the book from him to be sent by courier, and I received it in two days. It was a small book with only thirty pages. Prophet maintained that we each have the spiritual presence that resided in each of us, and we could all access its unlimited energy. In summary, she upholds that it is important for us to protect and sustain this contact throughout the day. She offered techniques that could help all of us to develop a close working relationship with God and experience the joy, peace and empowerment that are our spiritual birthright. This sounded exactly like the sermon I had heard in church, another book that I had read, a workshop and seminar I had attended, and a process I had gone through. It was all the same knowledge expressed differently.

I read the book in just a few hours as it was short, and I was done. As I was reading, my soul jumped for joy, I was in a state of pure bliss and felt one with everything. I experienced so much love inside of me for everyone and the emotion was intense. I felt like offering myself in service to others and in that moment I didn't have any problems, everything was fine, I wasn't challenged or confused, it seemed as if my past had been wiped out and it didn't exist, nobody had hurt me, and I wasn't needy or in pain of any sort. It seemed like time came to a standstill as I revelled in joy.

I then came to a deep sense of knowing and realisation that God is One. I had heard that statement before, read about it in books, but never had the experience of it as I did at that time. Reading, understanding and knowing are totally different things, which I had come to a point of comprehending while reading that book.

Being aware of the presence of God every moment of every day, and having the constant connection with Him is, to my mind, the cornerstone of spirituality. It summarises all the spiritual experiences a person could ever have. The awareness of the presence of God, I learnt, is something that needs to be cultivated daily, as well as keeping God in our thoughts all the time, while working, at school, while driving, doing daily chores and doing any form of service. You literally pray without ceasing, as St Paul put it (Thess 5:17). Speaking to God throughout the day like a friend enhances this connection. As one pastor I once listened to said, 'God is closer to you than a brother.' I have learnt that God is truly not separate from us, nor is He separate from our daily living and chores. He is present all the time and we need to be in tune and aligned to the frequency of heaven all the time to live a good and proper life.

"If I go up to the heavens, You are there; if I make my bed in the depths, You are there." (Psalm 139:8) Prayer is indeed an awareness and acknowledgement of God's presence.

God is not a God of a particular tribe, religion or race, He is the mother and father of all humanity, and that was a wonderful revelation to me. As souls, we are all here on Earth to serve a particular purpose, a divine and higher calling, and God, as the Creator of man, communicates with His offspring using any method available.

We all have the Presence of God, which the book referred to as the Higher Self, that keeps watch over us through major and minor calamities. It is a source of our inspiration and strength, and for me, whenever I became aligned with that Presence, I drew to myself everything I desired. Everything that I've ever wanted or could want has always been available in the alignment with God, whichever way I pursued it.

I have been touched by God in so many ways; wherever I went, God has been there too. Someone once said that he couldn't keep up with God because He was always a step ahead.

I came to a decision that I would not crucify myself but embrace all kinds of connections and encounters with God, whichever way they presented themselves. Different things worked for me at different times and I would do what worked for me at that time.

If I went to a prayer meeting and experienced God, and then meditated and still experienced God in that too, then I would embrace both experiences and enjoy them.

If I submerged myself in my gratitude journal and then took time to visualise how I would like to experience my reality, I would enjoy that as well.

If I went to any place where God was talked about and connected with God there, then I would enjoy the moment to its fullest.

If I have a vision in a flash and dream wholesome dreams, I would wake up joyful too.

If I go to therapy and workshops and receive a breakthrough, I will rejoice in the breakthrough as a gift from God.

These are the intricacies of God and how He chooses to appear to individuals is phenomenal. I deduced that as humans we tend to judge the things that we do not understand and draw conclusions, rationalising the ones we prefer and believe. This could be associated with our social contrasts and constructs, mental beliefs, experiences and training. The greatest gift that God has ever given to mankind was the gift of free will, the power to choose and thus create a society that is grounded in love and tolerance as we choose to embrace each other.

9

IT IS NEVER THAT BAD

"Trust yourself. You know more than you think you do."
Dr Benjamin McLane Spock

I had worked at my job for five years and was confident that I knew it well enough to do anything that was required of me. I had taken many business trips, had executed many projects, and began to ask myself what else there was for me until one afternoon I received a phone call from another colleague at work.

"Hi, Kgali, could you please come to my office? There's something I'd like to talk to you about." That was Melvin.

Melvin and I had a good working relationship, and he called me Kgali as most of my friends did.

"Okay, I will be there in a few minutes," I replied.

I was busy typing a memo to the procurement section about my orders for stationery, and felt that I could use a break. I closed my office door, locked it and rushed to his office, which was on the ground floor. I knocked on the door and heard a loud voice say, "Come in." As I opened the door, Melvin was on the telephone and he signalled that I should come in. I sat on the chair, made myself comfortable and started looking around his office. He had a beautiful portrait of the sea at sunset. He hung up the phone and gazed at me.

"Hi, Kgali, how are you this morning?" he asked.

"I'm well, and how are you doing?" I replied.

"Couldn't be better," he said.

I pulled the chair closer to the table and asked him why he wanted to see me, and he said, "I will be going away for a few days and was wondering if you would be able to stand in for me during that period. I can show you the things that need to be done while I'm away; it's not a lot."

I was surprised to hear the news, and wondered why he had chosen me specifically and nobody else. I was glad, though, as I would be doing something different from my usual work and thought that this would be a great opportunity to learn at a supervisory level. I sensed that I was ready to take up another position in the company, or even move to another firm if an opportunity presented itself. I spent the entire afternoon with him, as there were letters to shareholders that had to be written and I trusted myself to do that job well.

I had known Melvin for over two years; we often met at meetings and had brief conversations. I had never thought that he noticed me or my work particularly. I would consult with him at times for certain projects, but that is where it ended. I had to spend a week with Melvin before he left for his trip. He took me through the different reports that needed to be compiled daily and sent through to headquarters, gave me a list of people I had to call and arrange meetings with, as well as details of a number of other activities I needed to attend to. I wrote everything in my diary to ensure that I executed those things to perfection.

Before he departed, he left me with the keys of his office as it was easier for me to operate from there. All the resources that I needed were readily available, including the files that I needed to access. I spent every day behind my desk, ensuring that I completed all requirements to the full. It was an easy and effortless week that passed by quickly, and at the end of my tenure I was pleased to feel that all had been done well.

Melvin returned from leave after the scheduled week and we arranged a meeting so that I could provide him with feedback. There had not been any drama and everything had gone smoothly. I appreciated the new environment and responsibilities and more so that my manager had allowed me to assist elsewhere without any reservation. She trusted me and the quality of work I produced and knew that I would be available when required for anything pertaining to my normal duties. Melvin's work was stimulating and kept me productive and engaged the entire day. I went back to his office on my return and continued with my normal duties. I was a pro and knew most of the requirements off the top of my head. I also knew that when that occurred, it was time to explore other things. I had reached the upper limit.

It was in the sixth week that Melvin called me again to his office, this time to inform me that he had been offered a management position in another branch in the company and was relocating, and he thought that it would be good for me to assist in his position until someone new was appointed. I was astounded, as this just came out of nowhere and was something I never thought would repeat itself. I had only assisted him for a week and didn't know much about the section he was working in, and now relieving for an indefinite period was a lot, but something to be considered carefully.

"This is a great opportunity for you," Melvin said. "Besides, you are qualified for it".

At home that night, I went through the events of the day and thought hard about Melvin's proposal.

As I had been reading about the law of attraction and applying the teachings in my life, I was seeing the fruits of my thoughts and positive attitude. I needed a change of environment and new challenges, and the opportunity was now presented to me in a way that I had never expected. God was working miracles and wonders in my life, and the good things that I had been thinking about and hoping would happen were manifesting themselves in unanticipated ways. I took out my gratitude journal and recorded this as one of the blessings of the day. I sang like David, the psalmist in the Bible, who said that goodness and mercy were following him wherever he went and with God they overshadowed him always.

I woke up early the next morning feeling joyful and peaceful. I had been offered the opportunity of a lifetime and I had decided to gladly accept it. I called Melvin when I reached the office and informed him that I would give it a try.

He had only a month to transfer the skills to me, but first he needed to write a motivation to my manager for my release as the anticipated term of service in his division was lengthier. The recruitment processes always took longer than required. I had an understanding manager who cared for the development of her staff, and as long as I would avail myself when she needed me, we were all set.

I spent most of the mornings watching and learning from Melvin, and in the afternoon would retreat to my office to see if my manager needed me. Although I tried to absorb as much as I could in a month, the work was challenging and demanding. He had given me the easiest tasks to do when I had relieved him for a week, most of them being administrative, and this time my analytical and creative abilities had to surface. I began to doubt if I had made the right decision. It was the longest month I have ever had.

Melvin relocated to another city at the end of the month and I assumed his duties in the beginning of the following month. I believed in my heart that God had ordained this move, and as a student of the law of attraction I had to believe that everything would work out with God's help.

On the first day on the job, I had endless phone calls, requests from other departments, meetings to attend and numerous emails to respond to. It was hectic! It went on in the same way for the entire month. Things were not going the way I had envisaged; I had too much ground to cover and as I was still trying to familiarise myself with the rest of the functions, I began to feel that I wasn't coping very well, and gradually fear crept in.

I remembered the account in the Bible of Peter, a disciple of Jesus, who had seen Jesus walk on the water one windy day and requested that He give the word that he should join Him. Jesus told him to come and he got out of the boat, walked on the water and came towards Jesus. But when he saw the wind, he became frightened and began to sink. (Matthew 14: 25-30)

I was like Peter at that time, the violent winds of labour were sweeping me and I could not cope with the storm, and so I cried out to God, like Peter, to save me as I was fearful of drowning. I had been enjoying the fruits of my good thoughts relating to my prior job for some time, being fearless and carefree, and now the storms of life were rocking my comfort zone.

I regained my wits and reminded myself that God was with me and has always been. He had shielded and protected me in many situations and He had never failed me. His love and grace would abound all the time in my life. I knew at that moment that I was being prepared for greater things. My character had to go through fire, I had to be strong and apply my faith.

I went home fatigued every day and would plunge on to the sofa with my shoes still on. I would curl up like a baby and take a fifteen-minute nap before doing anything. It worked all the time, as it had worked for me when I was on maternity leave. All I needed was just a fifteen-minute nap in the afternoon before the baby woke up.

I listened to a pastor preaching on television one day and he said that there was a woman who once came to him complaining about the difficulties she was going through, and his response to her was: "Thank God that you are going through them as that means you are going over to the other side."

I continued with my work, giving all I had and sometimes I

went early to the office to pray for guidance and catch up with some of the activities that I hadn't finished the previous day. I felt stupefied at times, and couldn't even bring myself to plan my daily activities, as things cropped up from the moment I walked into the office. The harder it got at work the more I prayed. I intensified my prayer life but would wonder if I was missing the communication from God, the guidance He was giving. I knew in principle what I had to do and that was to listen to my intuition. I had to sit in meditation following prayer, but my mind would wander around and I was impatient. "Perhaps I am trying too hard!" I would think. At times I would wonder if I had lost my connection with God and had to find alignment again. At other times, I would try to rationalise and come up with reasons why I thought things were happening the way they did, but knew that I would never crack it if I was operating from a fear-based mind.

The end of the year came, ushering in the beginning of a new year. I never made New Year resolutions; they were pointless to me as most of the people I knew broke them. Going to the gym was a favourite amongst my girlfriends, and every time they would go for a few months, and then stopped going.

The commitment that I made to myself annually was to seek God more, and have an even deeper relationship with Him. My union with God helped me to retain my sanity, while keeping me focused all the time, and it still does. I couldn't imagine my life without Him and still can't. It would have been a complete disaster. I would sit in prayer and thank God for all the experiences that I've had in life, good and bad. The challenges had benefited me too.

I spent most of my New Year celebrations at church. It was the safest place around town at that time of night for me, and beginning the year with God was a must. The church services customarily began at nine o'clock and finished around one o'clock in the morning. They were usually packed with people and it demonstrated how we all longed and hungered for God, and to begin our year right. In my single years I attended these services alone, but as soon as I was married, my husband accompanied me.

I spent the holidays with family and friends and went to work immediately in the first week of the year, when it was really quiet. Most of my colleagues resumed work during the second or third week of January.

I started on the Monday and left early to have some quiet time with God in prayer for the New Year, and to have a marvellous journey at work. I knew that challenges would be there again as usual, but I prayed for the strength to deal with them effectively under God's grace. After my prayer, I felt at ease and serene and this continued throughout the day. I loved the way I was feeling, in harmony with myself and the world around me. It was a good feeling indeed that enabled me to complete all tasks smoothly and easily. I felt creative and happy. The day passed quickly and I didn't take notice of the time when I heard my colleagues say, "Goodbye, see you tomorrow."

It was time to go home and I still felt that I could carry on working. I was energised and the load was not heavy as we had just started the year. When I got home that evening I realised that I hadn't spoken to my cousin, Cathleen, for a while. Our last conversation was not particularly good and I was afraid that she was angry with me, and hence she was not calling. I was missing her and I went to my bedroom and prayed about the matter, asking God for a resolution. What surprised me is that minutes after my prayer I received a text message from Cathleen informing me that she was pregnant. I was amazed by the speed of God's response to my prayer, and that increased my faith that God is always on time every time. There were things that God answered instantly while others took a few days or months before being finalised, but the timing would always be perfect. I was confident in my prayer life and knew that with God I could conquer anything. All I had to do was just to walk with Him and never lose sight of what He had done for me, and that is what I committed myself to doing every day. God always came through for me and left me marvelling all the time. All that I have asked for, He always provided in His unique way, but the results were always appropriate and satisfying.

January came to an end and at this time the majority of my colleagues had gone back to work and everything had returned to normal. It had become a norm for me to go early to the office to have my special time of prayer. That morning I was inspired to resolve a conflict that had flared up between two colleagues on my floor. The two ladies had exchanged words and it had turned ugly. I called them to my office to have a word with both of them about how to treat one another at the workplace. They left the office having resolved to treat each other with respect, although I could see that they were still aggrieved. I decided to call them in during the day again to find out if they were all right, and the sound of their voices gave me sufficient comfort that they were over what had happened between them. I gave thanks to God for the opportunity to assist, knowing that this knowledge would be handy in my life as time went on. I knew that most conflicts were resolved through communication and mutual respect. If people humbled themselves and apologised, often there was nothing to resolve. Apostle Paul summed it up perfectly by saying that we need to be completely humble and gentle, be patient and to bear with one another in love (Ephesians 4:2).

I was proud of myself, knowing that, despite the challenges of my job, I was able to help fellow colleagues and contribute in other people's lives.

As days turned into weeks and weeks turned into months, the workload began to increase in momentum. Projects were pouring in. I was attending more meetings and doing endless presentations. There were times when I didn't even take tea or lunch breaks and would find myself drained at the end of the day.

An email came through one day from the head of the department saying that we needed to fly in to Durban for a meeting. Nothing specific was said regarding this meeting, except that everyone was requested to come up with ideas to improve the section and all the other points would be tabled on the agenda that would be sent to us during the course of the day. My other colleagues had to fly in from Nelspruit and Cape Town. I waited patiently for the agenda, checking my emails every now and then, but nothing came through. I panicked, as I didn't know what was expected of us and what I needed to prepare. I then decided to call the head of the department to find out what the meeting was all about and if I needed to have a presentation ready with me. I picked up the telephone and rang our headquarters, where Phillip, the administrative officer, answered.

"Hi, Phillip, it's Kgalalelo here," I greeted him.

"Hello there, how are you?" he asked.

"I'm fine, can't complain much," I articulated. "I'm just curious about why we are being called to Durban. Do you have the agenda for us, Phillip?" I enquired.

"Don't worry about a thing; we just need to formulate a working document for the department; nothing much," he replied, trying to ease my nerves.

We spoke for a little while and ended our conversation. At the end he mentioned that he would ask the head of the department to send the agenda. I called on colleagues in the section in the meantime to provide inputs, and anything that they felt was relevant for me to bring up at the meeting. Their inputs came by email, but I never opened them; I had plenty of work to do that day, and resolved to work on Saturday to do some proper planning as the meeting was on the following Wednesday. I moved my focus from the trip and concentrated on the other tasks I had to accomplish in the office. By the end of the day the agenda hadn't been sent. I switched off my laptop and went home with the hope that it would be sent the following day.

Still nothing came through the following day. It was Friday and we still had two more working days before taking off on Tuesday evening. I believed in thorough preparation before meetings or any other project I had to undertake and did not appreciate not being informed properly about what was required and expected, and this was troubling me even though I knew better to invite God into all my affairs. On Saturday I took a drive to the mall to look for an outfit to wear to Durban. I had to look good and I always ensured that whenever I had to go somewhere and meet people, I was presentable. 'If you look good you feel good,' as the saying goes. I was reprimanded, though, by friends saying that this was the weakness of most of the women - always buying new clothes for every occasion. I still insisted on finding something for myself, going back to the stores on Monday afternoon and buying a denim skirt and shirt. I thought a woman can never go wrong with denim, especially at a meeting that was said to be informal.

When my alarm clock went off at 5:00 a.m. Tuesday morning, I knew that I was in for an interesting day. I was filled with anxiety throughout the day as I anticipated the meeting. I only had to catch the flight out of Bloemfontein at 6:30 p.m. to arrive in Durban at 7:30 p.m. The departmental meeting was scheduled for 9:00 a.m. the following morning.

I made it to the airport on time, found a seat at the coffee shop, and sat a while to await boarding procedures. It was overcast and a bit chilly outside, and I was worried that we could have a thunderstorm and might run into turbulence in the sky. A few minutes later we were ready for take-off and I switched off my phone. I settled in my chair on the aisle right at the back. At that time in the evening the plane had a few empty seats as there were not many people travelling to Durban that day. The majority of the people at the airport whom I observed were going to Johannesburg. The trip was uneventful and we had a smooth journey. There was also no sign of rain when we arrived in Durban. I was the first to arrive at the airport as the Nelspruit flight was scheduled to arrive fifteen minutes after mine and the Cape Town flight another fifteen minutes after that. I switched on my phone just when the plane came to a standstill, and was preparing to go out. I knew that my colleagues would call as soon as they had landed.

Delorise from Nelspruit was the second to arrive as scheduled, and Wendy arrived a few minutes later from Cape Town. We were thrilled to see each other and the meeting was the first thing we talked about. My colleagues were as blank as I was; it was unlike the manager to call us to a meeting without any details. We went to the car hire to fetch our rented vehicle and drove to the hotel where we were to meet the rest of the local team.

The hotel was in the city, so we drove quite a distance to get there compared to a shorter distance from my home to the local airport. Delorise was driving and we trusted the navigator to get us there. It was dark when we arrived at the hotel and, on entering, the porter hurried to meet us and helped us with our luggage as we went to the reception to check in. We were given rooms next to each other on the first floor and had to meet the local colleagues in the hotel dining room. Since it was already late, we placed the bags in the rooms and went to join the others for dinner. It was delightful to meet everyone and we spent most of the time talking rather than eating.

We left the dining table at 11:00 p.m. I was fatigued on entering my room and couldn't wait to get to bed. I usually slept early at home and it was unlike me to go to sleep that late. I took a shower and then communed with God before I went to sleep.

I woke up with my thoughts on the meeting. I tried to visualise a great outcome but it was difficult to hold that vision. I was curious and anxious about the day's event and couldn't take my mind off the assembly. I made it a point that before I left I should have some time with God and ask Him to take over. I knew that I shouldn't take things for granted and think that nothing much would be required of us. I took out the material I had brought with me and went through it before I joined everyone for breakfast. My trust was in God completely, and I relaxed in the faith that He would see us through and guide us to the best outcome required for the meeting. Everyone's contribution was required and to make our work efficient we had to come up with great ideas and for me, great ideas came from God, and so I had to ask for wisdom and understanding. The conference area was thirty-five minutes from the hotel and we drove again together, with me driving this time as the car was booked with me as a co-driver.

The traffic in Durban was heavier than I was used to. Where I came from, that kind of traffic was unheard of and we had shorter commutes. I had the courage to tackle that kind of traffic as I recalled an incident when I joined the company for the first time, and the manager had refused that I be collected from the airport in Johannesburg and taken to Pretoria for a meeting. It was the norm in those days to fetch people from the airport as the company had hired messengers. This was one of their responsibilities. I had to get the hired car and drive myself to the meeting. It was funny since I got miserably lost and ended up not making it to the meeting at all. I had to stop at a filling station to ask for directions afresh to Pretoria. I thanked God that day that nothing happened to me except that I was mentally exhausted when I arrived in Pretoria, and was sent back home on arrival because I was extremely late.

We made it on time to the meeting, ten minutes before it was scheduled to start. All the local people were already there, including our head of department who came with the early flight from Johannesburg.

We indeed put ourselves under unnecessary pressure at times only to find that there was nothing to be concerned about in the things that we feared, and which caused us sleepless nights. The executive opened the meeting and, after welcoming all of us, thanked us for having made the meeting on time. It showed respect and commitment to him. He had a presentation that he shared with us and requested inputs. He required all of us to participate and come up with suggestions on improving performance in the section. It was an interactive session that was not strenuous at all.

I appreciated the lesson that I was learning that day, and that was that I needed to trust myself and put my complete faith in God. I saw how I could forget who I really was in God sometimes and it was in times of difficulties and challenges where I actually had to use the knowledge that I had acquired through the years. This didn't come as easy as I had imagined, but I had to remember nonetheless. I was hard on myself because I always expected myself to perform well. I took God with me to the meeting but as soon as I was there, I forgot about Him and locked Him out of my mind. His love and mercy endures forever, however, and He was sitting next to me in the meeting giving me the wisdom and ideas to contribute that our executive appreciated.

We finished the meeting at 4:30 p.m. as we had to rush to the airport to catch our evening flights. It had been a successful and fruitful meeting that ran smoothly. We all left the meeting feeling that we had made a difference and had accomplished something, and that our inputs would be taken into cognizance.

Goodness and mercy were again with me and I felt the warmth of God's love as I sat on the plane that evening going home, and I rejoiced.

10

THERE'S SO MUCH TO WORK ON

"Trust the process. Your time is coming. Just do the work and the results will handle themselves."
Tony Gaskins

I was approached by the Human Resources Department to consider reducing my vacation leave days as they were excessive on the system. I had a lot of credit and therefore needed to go on vacation leave for at least fifteen days.

I had been working hard for the past few months and considered the offer to take some time off.

My husband and I had planned a trip to Middelburg to visit friends for the weekend, and this vacation leave seemed to have arrived at the right time. We had been longing for a holiday but time always seemed to elude us, and the weekend was ideal.

I had been relieving in Melvin's position for four months, and my time was almost coming to an end as well. Only two weeks were left before I could return to my own job, and no decision had been made as yet regarding the filling of that position. I was not too concerned during that period as I needed some time to get away. The predicament remained as neither the Human Resources Department nor the head of the department concerned gave any indication about the future of the section. Nobody informed me whether it was all right to continue or whether I should return to my old job on my return from leave.

I had worked in my own field for more than seven years, and a part of me was not too keen to go back to that same job, but, of course, I didn't know what the future held.

More tasks and meetings came through as I prepared to go on leave, and the last week was frantic. The thrill of being at home and the planned visit to Middelburg with my family, however, superseded the stress.

Though I didn't know what was ahead of me and what God had planned, I resolved in my mind alone to continue with Melvin's former job when I came back from leave, and wait for the next step to be revealed.

Finally, my last day came and that whole day I ensured that I sent and replied to emails and that everything was completed before I left in order to reduce the work load on the person who was going to take over in my absence. The day ended and I switched off my laptop and went home to begin three weeks of rest and relaxation.

The first day of my leave came and, during the course of the day, I began receiving phone calls from work.

I was inundated with office requests in the first few days of my leave and I felt as if, although I was away from work, I was continuing to work at home. My thoughts revolved around work and I was stressed most of the time as it was a new experience for me. With my previous post, my vacation leave was just that - no one from work bothered me with phone calls. I felt a lot of tension in my back although I was at home, and it was even worse when I was at the office.

On Friday morning my husband and I packed our bags and put them in the car.

"Are you ready to go?" my husband yelled as I ran back into the house to check if I hadn't left anything essential behind. I ran through the list in my head and hurried to my daughter's bedroom to check if I had taken all her toys.

My three-year-old daughter was already buckled up in the car, so I locked the door and said, "We can go now!"

Middelburg is a small town in the Mpumalanga province, approximately six hundred kilometres from where we lived. It was a long, sensational journey for me, with infrequent stops at different filling stations for us to catch a breath and stretch our legs. I had never been that side of Mpumalanga before, and being on the long journey meant that I could lose all my worries on the road and look forward to an incredible and peaceful weekend.

Reaching Middelburg in the late afternoon was reasonable enough, considering the stops and the toll gates on the road. We had a very welcoming reception from our friends, who had been waiting for us in anticipation. Since we were tired from the long trip, we all decided to dine in and let the kids play in the room. They had a five-year-old daughter themselves, and so having a playmate made things easier for our daughter.

I woke up refreshed in the morning with the zeal to walk around and see the neighbourhood. We were in a quiet area, and not that many people could be seen walking around outside in the street, and nor did I see the neighbours. As in any other small town, there was not much to expect and therefore we spent the two days indoors, watching movies and having a braai, which is a popular South African term for a barbecue. The weekend was indeed relaxing and warm, but we had to go back home first thing Monday morning as our friends had to go to work. We said our farewells and hit the road.

An hour into our trip a call came through, and when I looked at the phone, it was a number from the office.

"I wonder what seems to be the problem this time," I thought as I answered, feeling a little agitated.

"Hello, Kgali, I'm sorry to disturb you," the voice on the phone apologised.

I quickly recognised that voice to be Delmarie, and replied,

"No need to worry - what can I do for you?"

"I heard you are on leave, so I thought I should inform you that that position you've been relieving in has been advertised; the advert just came through now and will be closing soon," Delmarie continued.

"Oh, really," I replied. "Thank you, Delmarie, you are a true friend. I will put in my application."

"All right then, let me not disturb you any further on your vacation. I will see you when you get back," she remarked.

"Okay, beloved, thanks again," I said, and hung up.

I was surprised to learn about the advert, as I hadn't heard anything when I left, and the head of the department never hinted that he would be advertising soon. So I guessed that I had found the answer to my question about the head's intentions regarding the section. God had once again used someone who never crossed my mind in a million years. Delmarie worked in the supply chain section and we hardly spoke to each other except when I needed stationery for the office. All of our orders were released by her section. It was unthinkable that someone like her, who hardly knew me, would call me on leave, but not impossible with God.

I decided to go to the office when we arrived home to email my résumé. It was six in the evening and I was certain that there wouldn't be many people at work at that time. I knew in my heart that I would be invited for the interview, as I had relieved in that position for some time and had the required qualifications, so I relaxed in that knowledge. I promised myself, however, that I would prepare thoroughly for the interview on my own, without really bothering anyone else. I was confident that I would find the relevant information on the Internet to assist me with the preparation.

I still had a few more days before my leave ended, and so on Saturday I went to the office again to begin with my preparation. I wanted to go to the office at a time when no one was there to avoid being seen and asked about anything related to work. There were not many people at work on Saturday, and only the security guards and the cleaning personnel. I knew I wouldn't meet them, since I was positive they would be at their work stations doing their jobs.

I obtained significant information on the Internet by ensuring that I searched for things relevant to the advert. Although I picked up a wealth of applicable information, I became anxious about the interview as I wasn't sure if I would be able to provide the appropriate answers required by the panel.

I also wondered if I would be the right candidate for the job and felt inadequate and doubtful. I thought about the environment, the people I had been working with, the previous supervisors who held that position, and the challenges I had experienced whilst relieving, and I felt overwhelmed. I had heard one supervisor make the remark that the position needed a strong person, and I thought deeply about that. My mind went to all other responsibilities of the position and expectations. I needed to come up with a strategy for improving performance in the section in case I was questioned. The office trip to Durban came in handy as I had written a few notes and understood the direction the head of the department sought to take.

I still had time before I went back to work and was confident that by the time I was called for the interview I would be ready.

I shifted focus and determined to think about things other than the interview, until I heard a message left on my mobile phone by the recruitment specialist. He had never called me before and it was quite obvious to me that he was trying to hint that they were looking at my résumé. On his message he said only that he was checking up on me, and I knew that was not true.

His voice alone made me nervous and it wiped out the little confidence I had left. I dreaded the call for the interview, but I knew it would come soon. I even thought about the possible dates for the interview. I had not been to an interview in a long while, and wasn't sure what would be expected of me and who would be part of the interview panel. My mind kept enlarging and expanding the picture. Fear enveloped me and my heart pounded like the throbbing wings of a caged bird.

I notified my husband about the call and that I was not sure about myself, and he cautioned me to take the interview seriously.

The thought of the interview stole my peace. I tried not to think about it too much and didn't want to hear from anyone who was likely to make any reference to the interview. As much as I tried to disconnect, I needed stress management and interview tips from someone or somewhere. I screamed from within!

I was shocked to realise how much fear ruled my life, and it was difficult for me, at that time, to focus my mind on God and trust that He would come through for me no matter what. To shift focus, I then decided to call a friend of mine who was on study leave.

"Hi, Bernice, how are things going?" I enquired.

"Very well, thank you," she responded.

"How are the studies?" I asked again.

"So far, so good. I'm studying hard and feel confident that I will pass the exams," she added.

"I know that you are a genius and you will make it," I encouraged her.

"So, what's happening at work? Will you be going back to your section after your leave?" she asked.

"I'm not really sure, because the boss hasn't said anything yet, but he has advertised the position," I said.

"Oh, really? Have you applied? I think they will probably hold the interviews at headquarters since it's at a supervisory level," she said.

I freaked out even more to hear that the interviews might be held at headquarters. I regretted saying anything about the advert, since I didn't want to hear anyone mentioning the word 'interview'. Anxiety got the better of me!

I cried inside for the times that had passed when I felt fearless and on top of the world, when I was mastering my own job and learning about the law of attraction and the science of the mind. I wondered where all this knowledge had gone to, along with the confidence I had felt. I kept asking myself, day and night, what happened to the good feelings, the peace that surpassed all understanding, the rivers of living water and the oneness and unity I had felt with everyone and everything.

I knew that I needed to get to that state again in order to make it through the interview, my job, all projects and my entire life. My state of consciousness regulated my life and I had to choose which state I desired to function in. I recognised that if I could gain control of my mind and never be bothered by anything, no matter how scary or trivial it was, I would have mastered my life. I knew that our lives were all about conquering our fears, anxieties, anger and all other vices until we reached the state where we can become like Jesus and become Christs ourselves.

In all circles of life we hear about people who resort to temporary pleasures in order to numb their anxiety, be it alcohol, drugs or one of many other things; mine was shopping. Every time I shopped I felt high and I found solace in whatever I bought, even if the pleasure was short-lived. As I matured in God, new clothing items or ornaments for the house lacked the excitement factor that I used to feel when I was younger, and therefore I abandoned the intended mission to go to the stores.

At that point I decided to write a letter to God.

Dear Father God,

I have been on the spiritual path ever since I could remember. You have always been there for me, helping me and guiding me. I have experienced Your touch in many ways and grace has always been with me. You have led me in so many ways and I attribute my life to all that You have done for me. I find myself constantly searching for just one experience and that is to feel Oneness with You all the time. I find it difficult to sustain that state though, and that is frustrating me so much. I know that Oneness with You means peace and harmony and I want to live in that state constantly. It should be possible for there are many who live in that state and invoke it at will. I can't be fighting and struggling all the time, there should come a time when the struggle ends. I know that You haven't called us to struggle and this to me is unnatural. I will be called for the interview soon, I know, and I'm supposed to be thrilled but instead I'm terrified. I feel inadequate and the feeling is tormenting me. There are many verses in the Bible that say we should not be afraid, but I can't help myself. Fear attacks unexpectedly and that drives me insane. I can't feel like I'm losing my mind every time something comes up in my life. Nothing seems impossible when I feel connected to You. I feel that I can conquer the world. The love and joy that I feel when I'm attuned are the emotions that I want to share with everyone, but I keep on going back and forth as a result of fear. One minute I feel the joy and the next I've lost it, and the cycle keeps on repeating itself. What should I do?

Many authors of spiritual writings have said they have had encounters with Jesus and others hear the still small voice all the time. Others even maintain that they've encountered their guides or the angels. They've all had these wonderful experiences and keep on experiencing them all the time while I, on the other hand, will read one book after the other, feel excited and, when I'm done, I'm always back to where I have started. Help me, Father, I am enjoying my journey for I'm learning every day but there should be a point where I'm able to encourage myself without necessarily depending on others. I know that You have heard me. Thank You for the answers to my prayer.

Amen.

I believed that God had heard me as I folded the page and placed it in my journal.

God has always provided for me, in His unique way, whatever I needed. It was soothing speaking to God any time and using any method that I felt comfortable with at any time.

I then decided to go to the office again to search the Internet for relevant questions and skills required for the job. I had agreed with my husband that he would take two hours playing squash and then on his return I would leave while he took care of our daughter.

I thought about the interviews for a junior position that I had conducted a month prior to the advert, and remembered a lady who had come for the interview; she didn't look nervous or anything but she was struggling to provide the relevant answers to the questions. I knew that she was familiar with the work responsibilities and had the necessary experience. I was saddened for the first time, as I understood how she must have felt during the interview. The panel had expected so much from her but I learned that innate knowledge and work experience didn't necessarily mean that one would remember everything all the time, as an interview is a competition and the tension that people experience during interviews sometimes clouds the mind. It is the same with examinations, where one can study very hard but on entering the examination room and going through the question paper, sometimes we seem to become blocked, or are anxious to finish without even reading the questions properly. I felt compassion.

When I was studying for the honours degree in Communication, we had been invited as a class to an evaluation of the thesis of a masters student. She had to present her research proposal to the professor and our team of honours students so that we would know and understand what was awaiting us if we decided to study further with the University. The candidate was also a lecturer in the department, and as soon as she concluded her presentation and the professor engaged her, she lost her composure and requested a few minutes' break. In her absence, the professor explained that even he became nervous sometimes when he was invited to be a speaker at major seminars, or to give presentations. He divulged that it occurred to everyone, even the most courageous of people.

I realised that the lesson couldn't have come at a better time. It never had an impact on me then when I was only twenty-one years old, but surely would come in handy in my time of need.

My husband and I received a call one day from a friend of ours with whom we used to go to church.

"Hello, how are you?" a soft voice came through.

"I'm fine, thanks, and how are you, Maureen?" I asked, yawning as I was tired from thinking too much.

"I'm also doing well, thanks. You sound sleepy," Maureen said laughingly. "I meant to call you earlier during the day, but wanted to make sure that all our plans were in place before I called. What are you guys doing on Sunday?" she asked.

"I'm not sure; we haven't talked about it yet," I said, rather curious about why she was asking.

"Well, if you are not doing anything, I would like to invite you guys to a farewell function that will be held for us at church this coming Sunday, since we will be relocating. My husband and I would really appreciate it if you could come. Do check your schedules and let us know," she requested.

"Okay, I will speak to my husband and will let you know if it is possible," I responded.

"All right, then, see you soon," she said.

"See you, bye," I said as I hung up.

Maureen and her husband were beginning a ministry in their area, as her husband, Brandon, had been ordained a minister. Their church had agreed that they should start a new branch fifty kilometres from the main one, as a need had been identified.

My leave was coming to an end and as I thought about

Maureen's invitation, I suggested to my husband that perhaps he should take our daughter and go to church on Sunday while I went to the office and caught up with e-mails in preparation for work. My husband agreed as he understood the challenges that would be awaiting me at work on my return.

On Sunday morning, we all prepared ourselves early, as my husband had to be in church at eleven. He first took me to the office at ten o'clock and then went back home to dress up and get ready for church. I didn't have the spare key to the house, so we agreed that, after church, he would pass by the office to see if I was done, and then we would go home together. He explained that his mobile phone battery was very low, so it might be difficult for me to contact him if I finished early. I was certain that I would spend the entire day at work and, therefore, didn't worry much about calling him.

On Sundays, the building was watched over by a single security officer, and it was rare that one would find other staff members at the workplace. I knew I was going to be alone in the building, and didn't worry much, knowing that I would make arrangements with the security officer as soon as I was finished for him to open the main door for me. I found the officer at the entrance when I arrived and saw that it was someone I knew and had talked to often. He smiled as I approached him. We greeted each other and he opened the door for me and told me that, as soon as I was finished, I should just come down the elevator to the ground floor, bang on the main door and he would open it for me, as he would be sitting outside the building.

I took the lift upstairs to where my office was, opened the door, locked myself in and switched on the laptop. There were many e-mails that I had to go through considering that I had been away for three weeks, and I stayed in the office until half-past-two in the afternoon as I assumed that the church would be finished at that time and my husband would soon be picking me up. I logged off the laptop, took my handbag and left. It was so quiet in the building; I imagined that it would have been a wonderful time for meditation in that stillness. I headed for the elevator, which was already waiting on my floor, pressed the button to open the door, went inside and then pressed the button to the ground floor.

The elevator moved just one floor and then it suddenly stopped!

I wondered what had happened as I tried the button to open the door, but it didn't work. I got scared pondering who else was in the building with me, and had possibly pressed the elevator button on another floor. I then realised that no one had called the elevator; it was stuck. I panicked and pressed all the buttons of every floor to see if there was any movement, but nothing happened. I tried to push the door open with my own strength, but I couldn't open it. I banged the door, but no one could hear me because there was no one in the building. I felt a cold sweat run on my back and my entire body froze. I thought, *'How will I get out of the elevator? There is no one in the building and the security officer is outside.'*

My mind went blank, and I couldn't figure out what to do. I then reached for my mobile phone, afraid that there might not be any signal in the elevator, especially as my battery was almost flat. I decided to try my luck, and called my husband; his phone was off! I then tried to call Maureen, then Brandon and, lastly, some of the members of the church who I knew had attended the farewell function, but all phones were off, and that indicated that the church service was still on. I tried to think again who else I could call and who would be able to help me, scrolled through my phone contacts, and Candice's name popped up. Candice was a close friend of mine from work, slender and full of fun, and I dialled her number.

"Hi, Candice, it's me. I'm stuck in the elevator at work and I'm scared; could you please call the guard and tell him. I'm terrified," I cried out.

It seemed as if Candice didn't quite understand what I had said as I mumbled quickly, and she asked, with surprise in her voice, "Are you at work?"

My heart was pounding and my hands shaking, and I was gasping for air as suddenly I couldn't breathe. I attempted to calm myself, and explained again to Candice that I was stuck in the elevator at work and there was no one in the building. She informed me that she would try to call security and call me back. I watched my wrist watch ticking over and waited in anticipation for Candice's call. She called after a few minutes, which felt like forever, and told me that the guard was not answering the phone at the security door.

"No, Candice, the guard is sitting outside; you won't be able to reach him; please do something, anything!" I exclaimed.

"Okay, I will call you back." She hung up the phone.

Minutes passed as I contemplated what to do next, whether I should try my husband again or just sit and wait. I decided to sit on the floor on top of my handbag to catch my breath and try to calm myself. I began to pray for strength and relief and asked God why this was happening to me and if there was a lesson He was trying to teach me through this experience. I was battling to quieten my mind and relax and I thought that if God did answer, I wouldn't hear the response as I wasn't connected to Him. After what seemed to be about twenty minutes, Candice called again.

"Hello, Kgali, I called Vincent, the head of security, and he said he would call the guard to go up to you, and will also call the elevator technician."

"Thank you, Candice, please check up on me again after a few minutes. I will sit and wait," I said with a sigh of relief that at least something was happening.

About fifteen minutes had passed when I heard the guard scream, "Madam, are you all right?"

"Yes, I am, thank God you are here," I said in a jittery tone as

I tried to calm myself.

"Don't worry, we will get you out; the technician is on his way," the guard said.

"Please don't leave me here alone; just stay right there until he arrives," I burst out even louder.

I didn't trust much anymore, and was happy that the guard was waiting outside the elevator. He just needed to stay there for me to feel secure.

"Don't worry, madam, you will be fine. I will have to go and open the door for him in a few minutes' time," the guard said with a chuckle in his voice.

"Okay, please hurry up," I responded.

I had been sitting in the elevator for an hour when I remembered that I had dreamt about my cousin, Cathleen, and decided to send her a text message with my phone to tell her about the dream. She responded immediately and asked how my family and I were doing.

'We are okay, but I'm sitting in the lift at work, stuck, waiting for a technician to open it for me,' I messaged.

'You are a workaholic and maybe God is trying to tell you to stop working so hard during the weekend and spend time with your family,' she texted back.

Something about her message clicked, as I had asked God what he was trying to teach me, believing that there was a lesson in that situation, and I had always believed that everything was in perfect divine order. I told my cousin that I would really think about that and not take her words for granted.

Two and a half hours had passed when I heard the voices of two people talking outside, and knew that the guard and the technician had arrived.

"Madam, it's me again; the technician is here with me and he will get you out soon," he exclaimed, sounding excited.

"Thank you very much; that means a lot to me," I called out from the inside.

I could hear that the technician was busy working, and felt the elevator move. It stopped on another floor. I had thought it would open, but it didn't. It was now stuck on the next floor and I panicked even more, wondering if the technician and security guard would know that it had moved just one floor. Fortunately, they had seen the movement and knew I had gone down one level. They both rushed to the next floor and tried to open the elevator from there.

Suddenly the door opened just enough for me to peep out-side. I saw a big blond man with a blue safari shirt and pants; he was pulling the door on both sides to make the opening big-ger for me to get out. The elevator had stopped in between the floors and I had to sit on the edge and stretch my hands towards him so that he could pick me up and carry me. I could feel the strength of his hands as he lifted me up and out of the elevator and put me on the floor. I breathed a sigh of relief and thanked him for saving me. I couldn't imagine being found the following day by everyone coming to work, unclean, and probably thirsty and hungry. As I went outside to patiently await my husband, I thanked God for rescuing me. When my husband finally arrived, I was happy to see him and couldn't wait to tell him the tale in the car.

11

Many Levels of Fear

"When you fear your struggles, your struggles consume you. When you face your struggles, you overcome them."
Louise Armstrong

I still had two more days before I could go back to work after my leave and thought that I would be called that Monday morning for an interview, but the call never came. I decided to find activities I enjoyed doing in order to fill my last days as I knew what was awaiting me at the office; besides, there were uncertainities in the environment I was working in. I spent the two days decluttering my house. I had read an article on the Internet about unblocking the streams of energy by clearing clutter in the house. I was a huge collector of all sorts of items that I kept in closets and cupboards but hardly ever used.

I cleaned up, packed things that I no longer needed away in plastic bags and threw away the garbage as well. They say that space says a lot about you by affecting your mood, your energy and your outlook on life. This was the best activity to change my temperament and lighten my spirit.

My home was also packed full of clothes, shoes and handbags that I barely used. I gave some of them to the nanny who was helping me with the child, and decided to donate some to the nearby shelter. I had the look-but-don't-touch habit, which was not smart as it created junk in all corners of the house.

The teachers of Feng-Shui say that clutter mirrors our emotional states and that if your home is cluttered, this would be reflected in you physically, emotionally and mentally. Clutter stops the energy flow in the house and creates exhaustion, stagnation and exasperation, they believe. (Wiley J, 2016)

I had been feeling exactly the same way lately and needed to see how far this activity would take me and if it would change anything in my life, especially the constant tiredness.

It took me literally the whole day to clean up, and even so I could not finish everything that day. I had so much stuff, and yet I was in so much doubt about giving some away as I went along that I had to decide the following day if I wanted to keep those items or not.

I felt an incredible surge of satisfaction after clearing my space. The house, including my cupboards, looked big and spacious. Fresh energy lit up the house and it felt airy. As I removed the shoes stored underneath my bed I thought to myself, *'I will probably even sleep better.'* I also figured that perhaps I should follow the same pattern at work by rearranging my office space and files and see if there was an improvement in terms of the work flow and clarity of mind. *'This I will do as soon as I go to the office,'* I contemplated. I wanted to take ownership of the new space I had decided to go back to in my mind in order to prepare myself for any possibilities. The thrill of how things could turn out to be on the one hand balanced the feeling of being too overwhelmed on the other. The possibilities were good, but I didn't want to raise my hopes and put all my eggs in one basket. It was quite perilous to believe and conclude that the head of the department would favour my application above all others.

Many a time people had made plans on their own and ended up being disappointed when the prospects failed to turn out as expected. I had God on my side and my hope was in Him alone. I believed that if it was time for me to take a permanent leap into a new position, then God would make that possible. Only God knew if I was ready and whether I would be able to handle a job of such magnitude. I received clear communication when I began from the head of the department to the effect that assisting in the position neither guaranteed appointment nor the extension of the exposure. There were processes in place and at any time someone else could be given an opportunity. The way I looked at things, however, there was no one with my qualifications in the section locally, and sourcing another person meant that the organisation had to look at other areas, depending on whether anyone there was interested. I also reasoned with myself that it would be costly for the organisation to relocate a person.

I went back to work on a Wednesday to be hailed by more emails, phone calls, meetings and plenty of problems to sort out. Before lunch-time, the usual feeling of tiredness returned and struck my back again. I took some time to think about what was going on in my body and tried to analyse the possible causes.

I knew that I was in denial and wasn't honest about the real problem that was causing tension in my back, which was stress. I was stressing about everything at work, I wanted to please my senior and I had bitten off more than I could chew. I was a perfectionist and everything had to be done just right. I had to prove to myself that I could do it, and prove it to my senior as well. I also believed that I owed it to Melvin too, who had believed in me enough to have given me the opportunity.

"Perhaps you should see a doctor," Martha said.

I had called Martha to pour out my heart to her, be candid about what was going on, reflect on it and, finally, find a way out of the stress I was causing myself.

The law of attraction states that we use our thoughts and feelings to attract what we want, and therefore to attract the state of mental health I required I needed to focus only on the outcome I wanted and feel my way into it as if I had already achieved it.

Proponents of the new thought teachings further argue that

we create our reality with our thoughts, that if we focused on the things that bothered us, we would create more of them. As a result we change our situation by changing our thoughts.

"I'm not certain, Martha, if that is the best way to go," I jumped in. "You see, I have been reading quite substantially about the law of attraction, and at the core of my being I know that I am the cause of my own stress," I added.

"I still think that you should see a professional," Martha was adamant and decided to change the subject.

"Tell me about your holidays then. You've been gone for some time," she continued.

I apprised Martha about our trip to Middelburg and all that I did during my leave. We spoke for a few more minutes, then hung up. I sat with my back against the chair in a relaxed position, contemplated our conversation and sighed.

Martha had a point, and although I knew what to do to focus my thinking, I also could see a doctor. I pondered. My body was aching and I considered visiting a massage therapist before making an appointment with the doctor.

I knew of an aromatherapist in town whom I had met along my spiritual path. She was the perfect person to give me a full body massage using essential oils. This form of therapy, I thought, would complement all the other treatments I would have.

I took my handbag from underneath my desk, looked for her business card, grabbed the phone and dialled the number to make an appointment. Rhonda, I came to know, lived merely ten kilometres from my home in a different suburb. She was qualified both in aromatherapy and reflexology and operated a clinic at her own house. She saw clients after hours and at weekends as well, and so arranged a massage for me the same day after work. Her home was nestled right on the corner of a dead-end street. There was not much traffic flowing into the street, which served her practice brilliantly. She had transformed a second garage into a health centre, which was separate from her family space. The yard was surrounded by trees, and near the entrance of the gate was a large jacaranda tree with a rich fragrance that pleased my sense of smell. It reminded me of an array of jacarandas that bloom in Pretoria during spring time, turning the city purple. You could detect as you approached the door that you were entering a homeopathic outlet. An assortment of aromatherapy oils was lined up on an open shelf, and the reflexology hand and foot chats were mounted on the wall.

Rhonda was a compassionate soul who listened with sympathy and understanding as I poured out my heart to her about my challenges while she prepared her kit. We then started with the massage in quietness and this lasted forty-five minutes until I heard the sound of the timer click and knew that we were finished. I got up from the massage table bed, dressed, and Rhonda walked me to the car that was parked outside her yard. My entire body was oily, including my hands and legs. I climbed into the car, switched on the ignition and went straight home.

On Saturday my husband suggested that we take our daughter to the zoo so that I could focus my mind on something else. The first thing that came to my mind was that there would probably be a snake gallery, and snakes were not my cup of tea. The trip, however, was not about me and my fears but to have an outing with the family and entertain our daughter above all else.

I woke up feeling joyful that morning; it was a warm spring day and the birds were chirping in the trees outside. The sky was perfectly blue and there was no sign of rain clouds gathering on the horizon. It was good weather for a day out in the sunshine.

I put our daughter in the bath tub, and she seemed excited about going to the zoo although I doubted whether she understood or anticipated what she was going to see there. I tried to animate for her in the best way that I could whilst splashing the water around, and her sweet chuckle told me what I needed to know.

I took her out of the bath, wrapped her in a towel and carried her to the room to dress her up while reciting all the animals she would see at the zoo. She sounded satisfied with the line-up.

I then packed a picnic basket for us, took a blanket and we went to the zoo. It was a short twenty-minute drive there, and as we approached I saw a few cars had already arrived at the parking lot. I was surprised as I had not realised that the zoo was such a popular entertainment spot. The one and only time I remembered being at the zoo was when I was seven years old. We had been visiting relatives in Pretoria when our parents decided that we should spend the day at the zoo. I had a vague memory about the atmosphere and the animals I had seen. This was only the second time I had gone as an adult and the idea was agreeable to my thoughts as well. We stood in the queue for the tickets, which to my surprise cost very little.

I felt a twinge of excitement when I entered. It was spring time and the flowers were blooming, people moving in one accord, dressed colourfully for the occasion, and you could hear the sounds of various animals in the background. We moved lei-surely from one point to the next, stopping at every compound housing the animals. We could hear the monkeys screaming at the top of their lungs. I looked at my daughter tucked nicely on my husband's neck with wonder in her eyes as we walked down the pathway. I had an amazing view of the giraffes and thought they must be the tallest animals I had ever seen. The ostrich ran wild, while the king of the jungle rested lazily in a cage. The chirping of the birds welcomed us as we entered the bird cage. There were different species of birds with beautiful colours to behold. I stood in awe of God's creation as I observed birds with different feathers and colours. We entered the aquarium on the other side of the zoo and all kinds of fish acknowledged us, big and small.

It was a fantastic stroll and view for the better part of the day and we were ready to go home when my husband said, "Oh! I haven't seen any snakes yet; we have to look for the snake park."

I have always been afraid of snakes and I couldn't even watch them on television.

I thought, *'Oh-oh, here we go; the moment has come!'*

He spotted the snake gallery and said, "Come on, let's go. We can't leave this place without seeing any snakes."

What looked like a cave was dark inside as we peeped through the window.

My husband then opened the door and entered, and I followed him. The snakes were all inside an enormous glass tank, so I took a deep breath and breathed out as I froze in fear.

I had never had any negative experiences with snakes at all before and since I was unable to attribute my fear to any particular experience, I couldn't explain why I was afraid of snakes. Most people and counsellors believe that to get rid of a phobia you need to be exposed to the object of your fear. I needed to be exposed to the actual snakes in order to overcome my fear. I then realised that going to the zoo that day was not only about reconnecting to the peace that was eluding me, but also to remove a layer of fear that was holding me back. A cousin of mine compared the process of healing to the act of peeling an onion, saying that there are different layers of an onion and when you remove the first, another one shows up and makes you cry. So we need to keep on peeling the layers of our emotions and fears until we stop crying because that which is at the core of our being is pure love, peace and joy. I realised that it was the day of healing a certain level in the soul and the opportunity had presented itself. I recognised this as a demonstration of the massive amount of work I needed to do in order to come to a point of complete freedom in my mind.

I approached the tank and saw snakes crawling around that made my body cringe. I had been taught at one of the metaphysics classes I had attended in the past that when you come into contact with anything you are fearful of, you should feel the fear fully, identify even the area of the body that is affected by the emotion, and stand still. When you become one with the emotion and do not try to run away from it by ignoring it, then it disappears. I learnt that you need to befriend your emotions and your mind because you cannot run away from yourself, as wherever you go, they are there too.

So I stood there and stared at the snakes, not even once moving my eyes as I felt the fear move in my legs and up to my torso as it consumed my entire body. I remained there without making any movement. I stood there long enough to feel the fear pass through me and then disappear.

I shifted my focus to the other side of the gallery where there were anacondas and slowly approached the tank until I spotted one that I pointed out to my husband.

"Look at that one," I exclaimed.

"How did you do it?" My husband looked at me in astonishment. "I thought you would be afraid and crumble," he proclaimed. He was amazed at how calm I remained.

"It was a divine appointment," I said. "I told myself when we entered that it was time for me to confront that fear, and I did it," I uttered with confidence and a sense of achievement in my heart.

"But you never appeared to be afraid; if someone saw you, they would have thought you liked snakes. Well, you should take a bow; I am really amazed!" my husband proclaimed.

We left for home soon afterwards and on the way I thought about how courageous I had been, as I confronted the phobia without pushing it away. It was a major accomplishment.

It dawned on me that I should approach all fears the same way in future and never push anything away as all emotion was a part of me.

I felt no need to make a doctor's appointment anymore as the massage had worked. My body felt better and I understood that I had to continue to change my outlook on life by working on my mind constantly and improving my thinking pattern.

I took another business trip soon after but this time to Pretoria for yet another meeting. The section was abuzz with meetings as high performance was the name of the game. Every organisation, though, depends on its employees providing a quality service to its customers, and it was a business imperative to keep on engaging and ensuring that everyone was in sync with the mandate of the organisation.

I was getting used to the routine and the flow in the section and this consultation was just another gathering to measure performance and evaluate progress. I had learnt on my previous trip to put my trust in God in everything, no matter how trivial it was, and this trip qualified. I was to meet the head of the department, but wasn't concerned much about his intentions this time and never brought the matter up. I presented the progress report that was required of me and listened to my other colleagues as they also reported about their areas. We were on the same level and our challenges were similar.

It was a healthy and quenching engagement that ended late in the afternoon, when we all rushed to the airport to catch the late flights.

I continued doing the work with grace and humility until I received a call a week later for the long-awaited interview.

I prepared myself to the best of my ability, feeling confident in my abilities and the experience I had gained. The head of the department flew in early that morning, and arrived in time to conduct the interviews with the local Human Resources Department. My interview was scheduled for 10:00 a.m. and on that day I was peaceful, trusting God for the best outcome that would serve my highest good. Accordingly, I went to the interview room feeling relaxed with faith in God alone. I was ushered into the conference room where there were only three panellists. They were people I knew and that made things even easier for me. I felt grateful that I had done a thorough research and had prepared myself well. I rejoiced in the Lord as I came out feeling unscathed.

Although some of the questions were beyond my comprehension and expertise, the interview had gone well and I was relieved that it was over.

I went back to the office an hour later feeling victorious. I had no desire to continue with my daily operations as the interview had consumed most of my energy, and I was mentally and physically exhausted. I had to remain at work, however, as it was still early and operations had to carry on. I tried to concentrate, but could not. My mind started racing to the job specifications themselves, because although I was familiar with a number of things, there was still more to learn. I entertained the thought that I could be the next in line to be appointed. I could actually be the new supervisor in the section. I imagined the event of receiving a phone call from Human Resources announcing my appointment. I stayed with the vision while feeling good about it. I thought about how the job would impact my life if I was the successful candidate. My focus was on this the entire day, and I concentrated less on what I had to do for the remainder of the day. There were other candidates who had come for the same interview but I was not bothered much about them, because what was critical was how I was feeling on that day. I had a gush of positive emotions that was uncontrollable. The feelings of contentment and joy overtook me. I lay back on my chair, closed my eyes and smiled.

12

THE BLESSING OF EASTER

"The highest condition of the religious sentiment is when... the worshipper not only sees God everywhere, but sees nothing which is not full of God."
Harriet Martineau

I was looking forward to my cousin visiting from Johannesburg for the Easter holidays. We had spoken about her visit often in our frequent telephonic conversations. Given was scheduled to arrive a day before Good Friday on the 9:30 p.m. bus. We spoke briefly that morning, as I had to attend a meeting. She had taken a day off to prepare herself for the road and so, unlike the usual call to the office, I called her on her mobile phone to confirm the time of departure from the bus station.

On that day I was exhilarated simply thinking about her trip, as the last time she had visited me was in 2004 when she had been experiencing difficult times in her life and was on a spiritual journey trying to make sense of things. She explained to me on the phone that it was a trip that she had to take as she was happy and fulfilled and understood her incarnation objective for this lifetime. She had been in a state of confusion previously when she came and, now that she had clarity, she presumed she had to pay her respect to the city that contributed to her restoration.

Given thought deeply about things and interpreted life's

events sometimes in ways that left me dumbstruck.

We had two sessions scheduled for our meeting at work that day, one in the morning and the other in the afternoon, when all departments had to present their mid-year plans. The day passed quickly, though, and since it was a day leading to Good Friday, most of the people at work left early, and I also left thirty minutes before the usual knock-off time. I went home to fetch my daughter before releasing the nanny and heading for the grocery store, as I needed to purchase supplies for Given's arrival. After shopping, I went back home to prepare supper.

I usually went to bed early, at about eight o' clock at night, as soon as I had put our daughter to bed, but this time had to linger a little longer as Given was arriving a little later. I flipped channels on television to pass the time until it was time to leave.

My husband and I went to the bus station just before 10 p.m. as the bus was delayed. On our way Given called, informing me that they were entering the city. We were still a bit far and knew that we would find the bus there already. We arrived fifteen minutes later and the bus had already arrived.

My husband stepped out of the car to look for her, as I was carrying our daughter who was fast asleep. They came back within a few minutes.

"Hi there, how are you?" she asked with a wide smile when she saw me.

"Hello, I'm great, and you?" I replied, excited to see her.

"I'm fine, too; your baby has grown so big!" she exclaimed. "I can see that she's sleeping peacefully, so I won't disturb her," Given added.

Given climbed into the front seat of the car as I was sitting behind carrying the child. We went home and by that time I was nearly dosing off as I was not used to being up that late at night. I had prepared my daughter's room for Given and when we arrived home, led her to the room. We decided to go to bed immediately as she herself was tired from the long trip. We had the whole of the next day to catch up.

When I moved from Mafikeng and Given ultimately moved to Johannesburg, it didn't stop us from communicating. We called each other as often as we could or alternatively texted each other.

We grew to be the best of friends over the years, and I guess neither of us knew, at that time, that this was a soulful connection, a contract we had made together in the spirit world, to stand by each other and grow together spiritually, as Jamal used to describe it. Jamal had taught me that when we incarnate we bring with us people who would help us on our path and draw to ourselves circumstances that would enhance the journey and in due course lead to growth.

The time had arrived for Given and me to discuss spirituality and things that we had been discussing only on the phone most days of the week.

We'd seen each other grow and develop in all areas of our lives, but nothing was more significant than seeing each other grow to the very highest level of our being, that is spiritually! She knew all about my journey with Jamal and the philosophy that had shaped me. On the other hand, I had seen her grow the same way too, using a different approach but all leading to the same God, the Supreme Being who fashioned the heavens and the earth. It mattered not which path we took; it led to the same source of energy that made us breathe every single day of our lives.

Discussing spirituality had always been at the centre of our conversations ever since I embarked on the journey. Given comprehended things in an amazing way too, questioning the building blocks of our societies, the man-made beliefs that influenced us, and before I knew it she was on her own search for something more. Our conversations as young adults had shifted from discussing dating to speaking about the deeper issues of life and questioning our own existence on earth as well as the reasons for our incarnation.

I woke up early on the morning of Good Friday, sat alone in the sitting room and meditated about what that day meant to me and the Christian community, including the entire Easter period, when my husband and cousin joined me.

I was raised in the Anglican Church and the activities during the Easter weekend were no different from other churches I had been to, marked by services on Friday and a series of activities throughout. The Holy Communion was prepared with the readings focusing on the passion of Christ. I would listen attentively as the reverend narrated the events leading to Jesus' crucifixion, death, resurrection and the ascension to heaven. On Sunday the message of Easter was recapitulated as Christ's triumph over death on the cross, and this message was at the centre of the Christian faith that Jesus Christ rose from the dead. I acknowledged all that I had been taught in churches and other religious gatherings about the Easter weekend. However, as I grew spiritually, I wanted more than just to listen to the recollection of the events, but also to consider the significance of that event itself and how it impacted my life.

We spoke about this over breakfast, and the exercise opened a new way of interpreting the events and understanding life.

It occurred to me as the discussion ensued that the significance of the crucifixion of Christ lay more in His resurrection than His passing, which I found mostly emphasised in the circles in which I had been involved. It was not the fact that Jesus was crucified but the fact that He rose again that was meaningful. I understood then that Jesus essentially came to demonstrate the truth that is within each and every one of us, and that is we are spiritual beings in human form and can live as He lived, and attain holiness as He did, and ascend to the heavenly realm to enjoy eternal life.

We felt as if we had been at a church service after an hour of discussion.

"This is really the kind of service I want," I declared.

"We didn't have to convene anywhere else; we only needed to understand that we ourselves are the church, the temple of the Holy Spirit, exactly where we are," Given added.

Given's words were profound, and we came out of our 'service' feeling refreshed and satiated.

The following morning, which was a Saturday, we took a trip home to Klerksdorp for the traditional ceremony of welcoming a bride to the family. My older brother had married, and in the African culture marriages are marked by rituals and exchanging of gifts between the two families. Every culture, however, has a unique way of confirming the marriage and therefore no definitive ritual or exchange is practised across all cultures.

In the culture of the Batswana people, to which I belong, when a man is ready to marry, his family writes a letter to the family of the woman and a delegation is sent to the woman's home explaining that their son had seen a woman in their family that he would like to marry. The woman's family would then respond by accepting the proposal and the negotiation for the bride's wealth, known as *magadi* in Setswana, would then ensue. On the day of the negotiations, which are done with the elders of the woman's family, the women who accompanied the men from the groom's family have to present the woman's family with certain gifts. In the African culture, once the negotiations have been concluded, that is considered as the marriage. Other people still choose to have another phase where they exchange vows in church by having a 'white wedding'.

The welcoming of the bride is yet another phase when all others have been concluded and the bride confirmed as a member of the husband's family. She is then given permission to participate freely and provide input on the activities of that family. The elders would then have another session with both the husband and the new wife, where they are told what is expected of them by their families and their in-laws.

I had been exposed to such a process when I was married and, going home later, I knew in essence what would transpire on that day.

We arrived just after 8 a.m., and my mother's kitchen was buzzing with young and older women who had come to help prepare food for the guests. Everyone showcased their traditional attire while the bride culturally was wrapped in a light blanket as a sign of respect and her hair was covered.

I observed as an exquisite united team of women in the neighbourhood and relatives worked together as one. I didn't even know what to do or where to lend a helping hand, as everything was organised and everyone resonated with one another perfectly. Being at home and watching all that activity, with everyone happy and jovial, was healing. I realised that I was meant to be there to receive the warm, healing energy that was the order of the day, and I allowed the event to embalm me.

I knew that God was there amongst us, dancing and celebrating with us. I believed that He was expressing Himself through everyone there. I watched as the event unfolded, people moving up and down and in and out the house as if I was watching a movie, and I felt blessed to be amongst all of them, young and old alike. The older women were ululating and singing African wedding songs. The neighbours came to see the bride as soon as they heard the wedding songs, and that is how we celebrated! We spent the afternoon with everyone and had lunch, and when the neighbours had left, the family was summoned into the house for another ceremony, where the bride presented gifts to my parents as a gesture of appreciation. I was seated at the back as the house was full and I had the pick of the blankets that were presented to both parents, a different pattern for each. This was yet another ritual unique to some African cultures as a way of bringing families together.

We left Klerksdorp at sunset and arrived home in the evening still full of energy, as we had enjoyed ourselves. Sunday was the final day of Given's visit, and she had volunteered to cook for us. As a vegetarian, she was to cook one of her specialities, and my husband and I were looking forward to eating something different from what we normally ate. We went to town to buy vegetables for the preparation of lunch and, soon after lunch, had another spiritual 'service', just the three of us. This time, we discussed issues relating to the healing of our emotions and how our backgrounds had a direct bearing on how we turned out. I recollected my school days and the ridicule that I had had to endure. I was saddened just thinking about the child I was growing up, scared and self-conscious about my looks, my height and my body weight. I had had to endure being made fun of and made to feel that I was not good enough the way I was. My husband often said that kids were the cruellest beings on earth; they don't care how you feel and they joke about anything and everything without any conscious awareness of harm. It was even worse when adults mocked you the same way, thinking that they were being cute.

As these memories ran through me and emotions began to surface, I recalled that I had to feel them fully, acknowledge and embrace them; they were coming up to be healed after all.

We were all affected by the events of life in various ways, we noticed. Some were similar and yet different. One of my favourite scriptures in the Bible says that: "…the sun has one kind of splendour, the moon another one and the stars another; and star differs from star in splendour." (1 Corinthians 15:41)

This reminded me that God created variety in all things, hence He made all of us different. We radiate God's glory in different ways.

We also discovered that despite the fact that we were all raised in loving homes, there were practices that we had picked up from our parents that we struggled with in our adult life and couldn't figure out why that was so.

For instance, when I was growing up, we were not allowed to

play in the house with our friends; we had to play outside all the time. My husband once said that if you aren't sure about how your wife would turn out to be, observe her mother and look at the entire family, then you will know. I always found that hilarious as nobody had ever told me that I acted like my mother. He said that with respect to cooking for instance, women cooked like their mothers because they were taught by them.

I never understood why I felt overwhelmed by many kids playing in my yard with my daughter. I thought that they made a lot of noise and they ruined my plants. My husband loved kids, and they always came to visit him. It made sense during our conversations that I picked up the habit from home. I appreciated what God was revealing to me during these conversations.

As we were talking I began to feel sick. I felt pain in my solar plexus.

I thought I had ulcers, and tried to recall what I had consumed during the day, but nothing was acidic or spicy in my food. The pain was unbearable and so my husband went to the pharmacy to buy some medication to relieve the pain.

"It might be that some of the emotions that you have bottled up for years are being released from your body," Given said, sounding so much like a spiritualist.

I had books about people healing themselves through opening up and releasing emotions stored in their bodies and wasn't certain if that was happening to me, but it made sense when my cousin mentioned it. The pain became better with the medication, but started again after a few minutes and I had to lie down.

I went to the book shelf to revisit Louise Hay's book: 'You can heal your life', and started paging through. Hay had a section in the book dedicated to describing the spiritual causes of illness and I had to find the cause for ulcers. She mentioned that ulcers related to a lack of self-love and not feeling good enough about ourselves, and I knew that was true. I had to affirm that I loved and appreciated myself, and I was good

190

enough just the way I was.

The following morning I woke up with that pain again; it lasted for the better part of the Easter Monday, and I couldn't get to a doctor as it was a public holiday. I set an intent to call the doctor the following day if I was still not feeling well.

We took Given to the bus station that afternoon, as she had to catch the three o'clock bus. We sat at the station until that time, but there was no bus available. We had misread the ticket and were told that the bus had left at three in the morning. We knew from our teachings that there was a divine reason for this mishap and my cousin never allowed that to ruin her day. We took her to the taxi rank, where she boarded a taxi. As we said goodbye to her, my husband and I felt happy that she had come to visit us and had been a blessing for the entire weekend. I'd had the Easter holidays of healing and reflection, and it was up to me to do what I had to do, to better my life.

The following day I was completely healed and there was no need to make an appointment with the doctor any more. I knew for certain that something significant had occurred in my body and in my life and all was well with my body and soul.

I had achieved much during the Easter weekend. The pain I had suffered in my solar plexus brought another lesson of self-love and self-approval. It is said that the solar plexus is the core of our personality and identity. It is all about the perception of who we are and how we feel about ourselves, and hence being confident in oneself was critical.

Secondly, as I had discussed with Given, I also appreciated that I still had a yearning to visit India. I desired to visit the spiritual head centre of the teachings of Jamal. He had often described the beauty and serenity of the place. It had meditation rooms where individuals could sit in silent contemplation, and lecture halls for daily teachings. There were parks for both play and silent walks. Every centre had white halls, the colour that represented purity and to make it easy for everyone to identify it as one of the centres. I saw this place in my mind's eye and dreamed about it often. I had pictures and videos I had acquired from Jamal and that I had stashed in a cabinet, and those pictures preoccupied me at times. I had moved on, had a family and my focus was elsewhere, but deep down in my heart I knew that I had unfinished business, and embarking on this trip would complete my joy.

I often thought about how to integrate Jamal's teachings in daily life with all the other knowledge I had acquired over the years, including Christian teachings. They were a part of me, whether I liked it or not, and I couldn't wish the knowledge away. It was stored in my subconscious memory and I had simply ignored it for a while but saw how it related to all the spiritual knowledge I possessed.

13

WE NEVER ARRIVE

"It does not matter how slowly you go as long as you do not stop."
Confucius

I went back to work on Tuesday after the Easter holidays, and every day I would think about the things I had to do emanating from the discussion I had with Given and my husband. I had been successful in the past in releasing issues buried in my subconscious mind through various healing techniques and knew that I still had more to release if I took time to reflect. I firmly believed that as soon as I had dealt with the deep-seated memories and beliefs that didn't serve me any longer and that were pulling me down, I would have come to the end of my struggles in life and have nothing to deal with any more. I also perceived this as one way of helping me to cope better at work and restoring my energy.

On Wednesday, I sent out an email to meet a team of staff members who were assisting me with the arrangement of a function that was soon to come. I scheduled the meeting for Friday at two o' clock in the afternoon as I had to go to a convention early in the morning of that day.

On Friday we met in the conference room as scheduled, and I was grateful that everyone had honoured the appointment and arrived on time. As a project leader, I had carefully selected people in different divisions whom I knew were capable of executing the tasks to perfection and were fully conversant with the various activities that I required to be accomplished. This was an important function for the organisation and we were expecting high-ranking government officials and the media.

I tabled everything that I required to be done by the team and invited questions and offered clarification when I was finished. To my mind, and in the presentation, the plan seemed easy and to the point and I never anticipated what was to come. I had opened a can of worms!

A hand was raised by a colleague who informed me that she was unhappy about how the past projects were handled. There was no proper coordination on the day of the events and we never came back afterwards to evaluate the results to see what had gone wrong and what was right. She said she was afraid that we might repeat the same mistakes and never learn anything, and besides, she believed that leadership should be rotated on the day of the event to give the others a chance to lead.

The first hand led to the second and then the third and all of a sudden everyone began complaining and agreeing with the first person.

I listened attentively as everyone raved, telling me exactly how they had been feeling with the past projects. I had been under the impression that I was steering the ship well and that our functions were successful all the time. I began to feel emotional during the meeting, but contained myself and gave everyone an opportunity to speak.

At the end every person had told me his or her views, and I thanked them for sharing them with me while putting on a brave face. The meeting was an hour long, and soon after we dispersed.

I was glad to receive feedback from the team while on the way to the office about what they thought about the other projects, even though that was not the initial intention of the meeting.

I took a moment to thank God before I continued with other activities.

I never realised how much I had been affected by what the team had said, and the following morning I began to go over everything that was expressed, and felt aggrieved. I began to doubt myself, as I had thought that we had a good working relationship together and good team spirit. I had believed that God had appointed me to be the team leader and assumed I had been doing a good job; even my track record showed that all events I had organised had been successful.

I felt restless the entire day and my peace had gone completely out of the window. My self-esteem had been knocked again, and I felt confused and off-balance. The following day came, and I still didn't feel any better. I tried to read inspirational books to raise my level of confidence, and listened to motivational CDs, but all in vain. I listened, but could not hear; my mind was wandering around trying to figure out what had occurred. I understood what the scriptures were saying when Jesus said that: "Whoever has ears, let them hear." (Matthew 11:15) Listening and hearing are two different things.

I became aware that we never arrive. When you think that you have reached a certain level of growth in life and have dealt with some of your emotional issues, other things come up and throw you off balance again.

I guess that had been the story of my life; I would be enthused by spiritual teachings or books, and every time I found something that made sense to me and filled me with joy and a pure state of bliss, I would think that I had made it, but my victory would be short-lived. I would continue to look for another book and seek another joyful experience, and I would really find it one way or the other. Most of my enlightened states, the states of complete bliss, were found in me reading a certain spiritual book. When I tried to stick with one that I thought was the ultimate, the pleasure would last for only a few months and, in the first month, I would live in a pure state of joy and peace and I would feel motivated and creative, but that would slowly diminish in time until I found another book to keep the fire burning again. I would even go to church, have a wonderful church experience, but as soon as I left the church premises, I would be back to the usual state of agitation, and then I would look for another sermon and then another.

Spiritual growth is a constant process. You never really get there, but you steadily grow, develop, advance and expand. Phases come and go and in every phase you learn something new. You increase your knowledge; you discover new things about yourself, God and life. All of these pit stops have signifi-cant value in your life and on your journey. Nothing is ever wasted, but it's up to you to grow consciously.

I went home, still feeling down and out of touch with the world. My mind kept racing back and forth and I didn't know what to do with what had been said to me. I tried to act as bravely as I could, but I knew, deep inside, I was shattered. I tried to think about the lesson in the whole experience, but I came out with nothing. I continued to go to work, trying as much as I could to act normally and convince myself that I was okay, but it was difficult.

The month of April soon came to an end, with the long Easter weekend behind and the South African Freedom Day in between, which is usually a national public holiday, thus mak-ing April a shorter working month.

I received a phone call on the last day of the month from Caroline, another friend of mine from work. Caroline was young and vibrant, but life had dealt her a hard blow when she fell ill and was hospitalised for a month. She couldn't understand how that had happened as she was an active person, but it taught her to take things easy and not to do too much, as she was also a workaholic like me.

She had called to find out how I was doing and if I had heard anything about the results of my interview a month before.

"Nothing yet," I said." The head of the department hasn't said anything yet and I haven't asked; perhaps you should call him as you know him better; he would probably give you a scoop, then you can tell me," I said, playfully.

"Just hang in there; perhaps something might come up in the next few days," she said as we ended our conversation.

I hung up the phone and took a few minutes to think about everything I had learnt at work since I began years ago and the time I had invested to ensure that I did everything right. That didn't come as a surprise to me as I knew I was a hard worker and was satisfied with my progress. I knew in my heart that it was time for me to make a leap, as I was confident that I knew my previous work very well and could add value somewhere else, either in the same organisation or another.

Whilst thinking about all this, I received a surprise call from the head of the department, who informed me that the results of the interview had been finalised, I was the successful candidate and had to start immediately with my new job. *Caroline must have known all along*, I thought to myself.

"Congratulations! You've earned it," he said.

"Thank you, sir," I replied, reeling from the shock. "I don't know what to say, thanks again," I mumbled.

"Your real work is beginning now, so make us proud," he added. "You will receive a new contract from Human Resources soon. Take care!"

I was overjoyed as I put the phone down.

I had been thinking about this for some time and finally it had arrived! I bowed my head and thanked God for the opportunity, as I knew He had everything to do with the appointment. I had entrusted my life and all its events to Him and He always came through for me. I had received a promotion and that was wonderful news that I wanted to share with my husband, and so I called him immediately. I also called my parents, as I usually share all my successes with them, then Martha, and then Caroline.

Everyone was cheerful, and I spent the rest of the day basking in the presence of God and His love as I thought of my new job. I gave thanks over and over again, thinking that God was always with me. Whenever I doubted myself and felt inadequate, God has always been there to see me through and let me know that all was well. I knew that, despite the criticism of my teammates, I was a great co-ordinator. Every event that I had ever organised had been successful and I needed to look at my track record and draw strength from there.

The head of the department had told me that he would come over to see me, as we had to go through the extra responsibilities that came with the position, and that made me a little nervous, but I was looking forward to having him in my area, this time as my boss!

He did not waste time when he landed the following week. I was glad that by the time he arrived I had read through the document that he had sent through to me by email, and we discussed it as this was what the meeting was all about. He mentioned some other activities that were a part of my promotion, and although some of them were unfamiliar, I saw the opportunity for further growth.

Although I had relieved in the position for a few months, nothing was easy during the first month of my appointment in the new job. Now that I was appointed, I was accountable and the treatment from the sectional head was not the same any more. I noticed that he had handled me with kid gloves when I was assisting, but now that I was appointed to the position, he required extra from me.

I had to be involved in quite a large proportion of projects, some of which I had to execute on my own, while others required working with a team of people. I was hopeful, though, that all the projects that were lined up for that quarter would be successfully completed. I had sleepless nights every night and went home exhausted as a result of the demands of the job, which included going to meetings, holding meetings myself, monitoring the effectiveness of the team, and so forth. It was overwhelming, even though I had experience in organising projects that spanned many years of working. There were many high-level activities that needed my attention and additional effort.

Suddenly things became totally different. I needed more people as the projects were massive. I had never done so much before with such a huge budget and whilst learning had never really made major decisions on my own without the head of the department's assistance. Responsibilities were quite extensive, coupled with the expectations of colleagues from other divisions. Within the first three months of my appointment I began dreading going to work every day. I also began to look forward to Fridays and would feel sad on Sunday nights, knowing that I would have to go to work again on Monday and face the same challenges. I always thought that being spiritual would rescue me, but then again realised that I had to go through another set of experiences, learn from them, learn from others, release and move on to the next level.

I thought that being in the new position would be easy and effortless, but there was no such a thing; I was still on the journey and the travel had many twists and turns. The road was bumpier and more slippery than ever before.

I would pray, release my fears to God, and take them back again by worrying and panicking; it was a vicious circle. I tried to remain strong each and every day, but that was a continual struggle and I was exhausted. I had never felt so overwhelmed in my previous job; I was more relaxed and would look forward to going to the office most of the time as the responsibilities were not that many. I had ample time on my hands to do everything within the day, but it was different with my new job. I would often take files home with me so that I could work from home at night and over the weekends. I had been under the impression that I would enjoy my job every single day when I began, and thought that whatever might change from my previous responsibilities, it wouldn't be much. The journey was getting harder. I felt as though I was climbing a steep hill and the more I went up the harder it became for me to climb.

I received an email one morning from Jade, one of the ladies from my meditation class. She informed me that her friend, who was clairvoyant, would be visiting for a while and would be staying with her, and if I was interested in having a session with her, I should book an appointment. I thought about her invitation and meeting an intuitive person seemed like a great idea. *Perhaps she would be able to reveal things to me that the hypnotherapist couldn't,* I pondered. I was certain that if she was intuitive then she probably could take me through a past life regression and so I decided to give it a try again.

I asked for her telephone numbers so that I could find out what she could do for me, prayed about the matter, invited God to help me and called her right away. I always ensured that I covered myself with the light of God in any kind of pursuit.

The woman picked up the phone and we exchanged greetings, but before I could say much she asked me if I had a grandmother who had passed on and was short in stature.

I said, "Yes, but why are you asking?"

"She is standing next to me, and she loves you very much," she said.

I was surprised by what she had just said, as I hadn't even begun to tell her why I had called and yet she had already stepped into the field of the spirits. I continued to listen with curiosity.

She then told me that there was another person in my family who was looking after my mother and me; he was our guardian angel who had come forth also.

I thought, 'Wow, I've got to make an immediate appointment and see this woman. She might have the answers I have been looking for;

she might just succeed in providing what I need and it is worth a try.'

I have always been inquisitive, adventurous and, to a certain degree, fearless, and I wanted to go back in time to my earliest memories, and perhaps even further, to previous lives. Various therapists have used different methods to heal memories and phobias and past life regression has been investigated at length as another modality people can employ for healing cellular or subconscious memories. This has always been an area of interest to me and when the opportunity presented itself to try again, I gladly took it.

I was looking forward to meeting the woman, and made an appointment. It was then Monday morning and my appointment was scheduled for Friday at 3:30 p.m. It seemed as if the week dragged on to reach Friday, as I was anxious about my appointment. Jade gave me directions to her home, which was about twelve kilometres from town. I told my cousin, Given, and my husband, and felt that was it; I would finally get my breakthrough and know how I related to everybody in my life and what I had come to this incarnation to do. I reasoned that I would know why I had to struggle with so many issues and understand the underlying factors to certain behaviours.

I arrived at Jade's house on Friday at quarter past three and was received by a mature woman at the gate. She smiled at me as I started to open the car window to greet her, but instead she opened the car door to usher me out and gave me a warm hug. I was happy to meet her and wanted to hurry into the house for my session. Jade lived on a farm with her husband and her father and the surroundings were peaceful and quiet. You could only hear dogs barking and chickens clucking while pecking in the yard.

I followed the woman to a room that Jade used for her sessions with her own clients, as she was also a therapist. She offered me a seat and told me to make myself comfortable as we were about to start with the session. She took out a notebook and a pen and explained the process that she was about to follow.

She looked at me again with a smile and said I should relax, while she started counting to ten as she eased me into a deep state of relaxation and I moved into the field of my subconscious memories.

"Well... I see a little white girl in the back yard... of what I think is her home. She is playing on her own... She's wearing, I think, a pink frock that ties at the back... She has black hair held in ponytails, with freckles on her face... Two black kids join her and the one starts playing with her whilst the other is just standing on the side... She's now in the house, as her mother has just called her. She is sending her to the store. I see her go out of the front door and run to the store; she passes a horse cart with two gentlemen wearing long black hats. The little girl has returned and is in the house again with her mother."

I heard myself speaking from what I was viewing in my mind's eye.

As we continued and she guided me through a series of commands, I started seeing further that same child in her teen years, wearing a school uniform, with her hair tied in a ponytail again. It was 1857 when the woman started asking if I knew what year it was. I couldn't continue from then onwards.

When I came out of hypnosis, I wondered if I had made things up or had really seen myself in a different context, or other people.

I left Jade's home feeling happy about what I thought had been a successful session. I made a commitment to book another appointment to validate the experience. I got home before 6 p.m. to find my husband and daughter watching television. I explained to him what had happened and that I had made an appointment for him for Sunday, as he had indicated that he wanted to observe, also out of curiosity, this particular technique. I knew that although my husband didn't believe in this sort of thing, we nevertheless thought the experiment was harmless. I had gone through similar hypnosis on numerous occasions and had come home just the way I was and how he knew me.

His appointment on Sunday was from 8 a.m. to 10 a.m and he left home thirty minutes before the appointed time. I was curious about his session, wondering if he would achieve anything. I thought about him while having breakfast and couldn't wait for his return.

He came home at around half-past-ten and told me about his experience, although he could not validate what he underwent and so I never really got much from him, except his opinion about the process.

I was not concerned much about my husband's opinion and respected where he was spiritually as I thought it's not everything for everybody. My journey had all the roadwork signs: *detours, road construction ahead, slippery road ahead, do not overtake, speed bumps, dead end* signs, and even *no entry* signs. I could never keep straight only. If I wanted to go back to where I had started, I would simply make a U-turn. The different processes were of interest to me at different times. I strove for what I could fathom and all of these propelled me forward. I kept track of whatever worked for me at a particular point in time and moved on when I wasn't feeling it any more, or when it did not serve the intended purpose. So I would move back and forth depending on what I needed and what lifted me up in that season.

I went for another appointment where the woman took me through the same process as previously and, to my surprise, I couldn't progress with the regression. She tried all the methods she could but still nothing happened. For an hour and a half I just stared at the darkness of my mind, not perceiving anything. I thought perhaps I had too much on my mind or had too many expectations.

We decided to end the session as I wasn't achieving much. I left the place very disappointed as I headed for the office. I couldn't believe that nothing actually happened. My mind started spiralling to the first time I had heard about past-life regression and the attempted sessions. I felt despondent that all of these sessions never really reaped the benefit I was looking for. I had ended the sessions not knowing if I had done them right.

I even decided to call Jade and inform her that I would not be going to the meditation classes for a while. Something I had believed in so much never worked for me; this made me disheartened and something within me gave up on this process. I thought that perhaps I shouldn't read or ever try guided meditation, or attempt hypnosis and regression any more. I was discouraged as I thought that now I would never know what I wanted to know.

I remembered an experience in church when I had seen people talk in different tongues, or languages, similar to an event described in the Acts of the Apostles in the Bible, when Jesus told His Apostles to wait for the baptism of the Holy Spirit on Pentecost, where they would be given the ability to speak in other languages, and this was so. Although I thought I could never experience something like that, when the time came and people were invited to the altar desiring to be baptised with the Holy Spirit, with the evidence of speaking in other tongues, I stood up, went to the front and received a heavenly language myself out of faith.

I knew that anything was possible to those who believed, and that whatever we desired to achieve we could.

I wanted to experiment with regression during that season in my life, but it didn't take me that far. I started questioning my own faith and thought that perhaps I was not ready, or God was not willing to take me through the process at that time. Again, another experience where I thought I would achieve something had failed, and I needed to proceed with my journey and see where it would take me next.

Nothing really improved for me at work, either; responsibilities increased drastically, work became even tougher, and there were too many engagements that I had to attend to. Keeping my spirits up and focusing on spiritual growth became harder until it was a great effort. I shifted my focus on to journalizing, but that challenged me as I would write a few things and then quit and prayer became a dreaded effort.

My problems at work didn't change or improve and sometimes I would even become agitated at home.

I decided to enrol for an online course in metaphysics; for a while I felt enthusiastic but my enthusiasm was shortlived as I couldn't complete the practical assignments, and meditation as part of the course became cumbersome. I would sit in my quiet space and thoughts would come and go, but the stillness that I was supposed to accomplish eluded me.

I confided in my husband, who would comfort me, but after a while I would feel miserable again.

I missed the times when I had felt optimistic and was at the peak of my game. I wondered what had happened to me and whether God had abandoned me. What was it about my life that was not working out right? I knew I couldn't blame anyone because these were my issues and I only needed to find a way of dealing with them.

I contemplated changing jobs to find one that was fun, enjoyable and carried fewer responsibilities. Having to take work home was not appealing, and it denied me bonding time with my daughter. I knew that those who had envied me in the position would rejoice if I resigned.

These thoughts consumed my mind for a long while. My metaphysics assignments included exercises in self-awareness, and I was honest in my answers. I felt as if I was spiralling down and I didn't have anything to hold on to.

I thought about the trip to India. I had sent a motivational letter by e-mail to Sister Charmaine requesting her to allow me to go to India with Jamal on the next trip as a guest, and to date had received no response. I re-sent my enquiry and shortly after she responded with an indication that the request was being evaluated.

I didn't see any improvement in other areas of my life, and sometimes felt sick to my stomach that I had been walking this road, yet at every stop that I arrived at there would be other things, other hurdles for me to deal with. There was too much going on in my life and my mind. I would have the confidence, then lose it again; have the self-esteem, then lose it again; love myself and appreciate myself, then lose that again. I would feel fearless, and then fear would creep into my life again and sometimes even redouble its efforts. I felt tired of trying so hard, yet not achieving entirely. I acknowledged, nevertheless, that I had made some progress in my life and had changed slightly; there were things that used to bother me that didn't bother me nearly as much any more.

I wanted to give up, but didn't know the difference between giving up and letting go, or surrendering. I didn't know exactly where I was, but knew that I was an emotional wreck. I had struggles and was troubled a great deal.

I began to suffer from backache again and knew that there might be emotional attachments there that were making me sick. I decided to go to a homeopathic practitioner, who told me that my organs were about to give in because of exhaustion and stress, and gave me medication.

I wished to put my hands on my head, sit on the floor and cry. I was emotionally exhausted and there was nothing that made me feel better. I would read a spiritual quote or listen to motivational speeches, yet these didn't help much. I felt that my confidence was bruised and felt lost and defeated. I didn't know what to do or which direction to take.

I began searching for a new job in the newspapers, submitted my résumés, and continued to do whatever was required of me each and every day, but without any passion or zest. I continued with the metaphysics lessons, but not with the *oomph* that was required. I kept asking myself if I was swimming against the tide and why everything was not going according to my plan. I knew what I wanted to see and the conditions I wanted to live in.

I found the strength to pray one evening and indicated to God the kind of job that I was looking for. There was fear, however, that, if I expressed this in prayer, I might sound ungrateful, and that was not the case. I just needed something that was more fulfilling, enjoyable and less stressful. I was also afraid that people would think I was crazy for leaving - and what if things didn't work out in the new job? I heard my mind chattering but told myself that I shouldn't be afraid of moving for fear that things might not work out.

I thought about how I met my husband and our wedding day, the birth of our child, my conversations with God, and how everything in my life had turned out well, and this was through the intervention of God and not the work of man. I knew that, if I believed and trusted in God, I could never go wrong.

I often heard people say that our organisation offered better opportunities for growth than other organisations, and that those who had left wanted to come back, but had to ask myself if this was the truth or just a perception. Was I going to trap myself and convince myself that what my colleagues had said was true? People had moved in and out of companies, and had progressed fairly well. I knew of such people. I had moved three times as well and had been all right. I fully believed that if I made my desire for a new job a prayer request, things would go on in a perfect way. I needed to let go of the desire and put it safely in God's hands and not even worry about the company I should be working for, because God would find the perfect place for me.

I didn't want to think about the possibility of that not happening, as I knew that would be my mind talking and not my spirit. In all spiritual books I had read, my spiritual heroes were successful people, just what I wanted to be. I knew that I had never struggled with anything in my life; all that seemed to be a struggle was just a stepping stone to better things, my life had been good, God had never failed me and wouldn't fail me this time.

I found the courage to open my gratitude journal again, jotting down all events that God had pulled me through, the gifts He had brought into my life and my achievements, so that I could refer back to them whenever I felt that things were not happening as fast as I had expected.

I've noticed that there are many people in this world who live great, secure and perfect lives and are happy. I've never believed that struggling was a natural way of life. I see fear as a contributing factor in delaying our blessings and keeping us from achieving the things we want to achieve in life. According to the advocates of the law of attraction, a person can have whatever he likes and still be able to handle any combination of circumstances with the help of God.

I saw the possibilities in my life and how great I could be, while advancing a little more every day. I believed that God, in me, was eager to do more, and I had to step out of the way and let Him do what He does best without my interference and fear. I had been trapped before by fear, when I removed my eyes from God and became derailed and delayed. I knew that there was a lot of work that I still had to do, an inner work that needed dedication and patience.

I decided to keep quiet about my issues and desires, as I didn't want to invite opinions from others and how they thought that what I was asking for was impossible and could not be achieved. It was my business with God, and I had to keep reminding myself of my track record so that I wouldn't lose hope.

14

You Can Still Affirm, Even If You Don't Feel...

"If you feel like giving up, just look back on how far you are already"
Unknown

I had been affirming for a different and more convenient job for some time and occasionally didn't feel like doing my affirmations as I wasn't feeling them all the time. I had learnt from many teachings that affirmations should be followed by an intense feeling to make them manifest quicker. I wondered for a while why I wasn't feeling any emotion, and why my affirmations were turning into useless routines. From time to time I would forget to say them. I would question myself and wonder if I wasn't dedicated enough, but wouldn't find the answers. I knew that, in stillness, I would hear the still, small voice in my soul, but every so often I was too lazy to find time for stillness.

At times, things would be revealed in my dreams. I kept my journal on the headboard pedestal so that if I woke up in the middle of the night or in the morning, I would write the dream down and then go back to sleep again.

I thought about the new job often and when I couldn't affirm its manifestation as a result of slothfulness I would feel frustrated.

The Sunday newspapers carried plenty of job adverts, and

on that particular Sunday I felt lucky and that maybe it was the day of my good fortune. I woke up early in the morning, cleaned the house and took a bath. My husband and daughter were still asleep at the time and I was feeling like I was on top of the world. It was still too early for me to go to the shop to buy the newspaper, so I decided to watch television for a while to pass the time. The store opened at 7 a.m., but the newspaper was usually delivered only around 9 a.m. and so I had to wait a little longer before I went out.

I left the house at 8 a.m. to go to the store and try my luck, and fortunately all the newspapers I needed were available. I grabbed them and rushed home. My husband and daughter were already awake and were sitting in the living room, wondering where I had gone to that early. I came home with two thick newspapers in my hand and sat to browse the career sections. I had bought the same papers the previous Sunday, and there was nothing in there for me, but this time my hope was high. I looked through them page by page, paying attention to every job opportunity advertised. I came across adverts for jobs in my field, but in other provinces, and I wanted one in my home town. I had listened to the pastor of the church I used to go to, who had once said that you could get a job wherever you were; you didn't have to move overseas or leave your home town believing that there was a lack of job opportunities there. I remembered the time I had visited a friend in London two years previously and she had told me that some of the people from South Africa were living there too, but due to the high cost of living abroad, they were forced to share accommodation, as the conditions were not as rosy as they had thought. Some were successful and were living the dream, whereas others wanted to go back home.

Thinking about that, I believed the pastor and hung on to his words. I had had a similar experience and therefore a testimony to back up. When I first came to town to pursue a career opportunity within a year I had moved to another fantastic job, and so I believed that another incredible opportunity would present itself.

Besides, I had a family and didn't wish to relocate. I was happy in that city, and it provided me with everything that I wanted and needed, especially a life of serenity and tranquillity.

I wanted to make changes in my life right there in that city and give back to the city I was living in something of value.

I remembered the pastor's words perfectly and clearly, and I convinced myself to look for job opportunities in that city and nowhere else. I kept this a secret from my friends as I knew that some would impose their opinions on me and tell me that my aims were not realistic and that I couldn't concentrate on one area when looking for a job. I also knew that most of them believed that a lot of job opportunities were only found in bigger cities, and not in my area.

I didn't want to be criticized and I have since learnt to keep quiet about my intentions to avoid judgement and discouragement. My only confidantes were God and my husband.

I paged through the papers, and the more I failed to find what interested me, the angrier I felt. I could feel the anger moving in my chest way up to my throat, and felt as though I could cough it out or throw up, but knew that it was only energy in motion and ways of dealing with it were different. My anger increased when I reached the last page of the career edition, and I was irritable. I went to sit outside, needing the warmth of the sun, as it was still winter, but then came into the house again after a few minutes and paced up and down.

"What's wrong with you, sweetheart?" my husband asked. "You look annoyed about something; talk to me," he said.

"Well, I couldn't find anything in the newspapers again, and I was so optimistic; don't great writers say you have to be positive and hopeful when you want something?" I asked.

"Oh, yes, you have to be positive all right, but you can't push the hand of God, and so you also have to be patient," he said.

That didn't comfort me, but I knew that he was right. I guess that showed a bit of desperation on my part that was not necessary. I only had to think about how other things in my life had manifested with God; some came quickly and some took time.

When you are in a difficult situation sometimes you forget; you hardly think about the good in your life and how things turned out for you. It's only when things are going right that most of us cite the hand of God in our situation and really notice that He answered at the perfect time. At that moment, I took the car keys, picked up my daughter and decided to take a drive. I thought I would visit a friend who lived in the township, but knew that I would be tempted to tell her how I felt, and I didn't want to do that. I wanted to contain my feelings and deal with my emotions the right way: feel them and then release them.

On my way, I remembered that I hadn't given my child anything to eat and decided to go to a nearby café to buy some food and a cool drink for her. As I approached the parking area, I could see that there was a security guard standing there, showing people where to park, but I was indifferent; I didn't even notice as he beckoned. I was in my own world and didn't want to be disturbed and so I found my own parking spot. I went into the café, bought food and left quickly. I wanted to disappear. I was very angry and disappointed, and yet in the morning when I woke up I had had a positive outlook on life. I decided at that moment not to go home yet but to travel around town to cool off.

Driving around made me feel better, and my anger and frustration subsided. I went back home after a while to prepare dinner for the family. I felt energised by the trip; it had been soothing and healing to my soul. I undertook to purchase all weekly newspapers as well and look for a job more vigorously. That was the new way to go, as I knew that I had to do something instead of just thinking that if I prayed and affirmed my desire for a job, one would just drop from the sky without me making any real effort.

Weeks passed and there was still nothing in the newspapers that interested me, and particularly jobs in my field. I sent out my résumé to all the recruitment agencies I knew, and also registered online. I was determined to do everything in my power to ensure that I was an active participant; God would make the right job available at the right time, at the right organisation, right here in my city, I believed. Months passed and still no positions, and my faith was tested. I re-examined my affirmations and thought perhaps I should wait until I felt really joyful to affirm again.

Whenever I didn't feel a powerful positive emotion, I didn't affirm. As time passed and nothing came through, I began to lose ground. I affirmed whenever I felt like it and when I remembered to. I went to a book store one Saturday morning and bought another book on the law of attraction, in which the author specified that sometimes we delay God by not doing our part and being discouraged too quickly. The author also mentioned that God was a perfect gentleman, allowing us to think through our desires and letting us change them as much as we wanted, so that we could be very clear about what we desired.

I thought about those words for a few days, realising that perhaps my vision was not clear enough, and thus decided to work on adding details to my affirmations. I was led to watch a religious programme on television one day when I heard a pastor say that we don't have to 'feel in order to persist in prayer'. That was a revelation for me, as I realised that I wanted to feel good every moment of each day for me to affirm. I recognised that I could continue to affirm, even if I didn't feel like it. I could pray, even if I didn't feel like it, and even more when I was led to. Not affirming at all or praying because I didn't have the associated feelings made me regress. It made me lazy and led me to affirming only occasionally. A week would pass sometimes when I didn't feel like affirming. Sometimes I would come home tired because of the demands of my job, and sometimes someone would have upset me and I would just go to bed without doing my affirmations or praying.

The good news was that I was consistently in communion with God, and knew that I could talk to God as honestly as I could. I didn't have to censor my words or structure them in a certain way, since all that was required was speaking to God with complete sincerity about how I was feeling. I had to remember that God was my best friend, closer to me than even my hand, and understood how I felt even before I could say anything to Him. God had the ability to handle any combination of emotions and events in my life and even when I felt my communication had to be structured in a certain way, it was really not necessary as long as I kept on going. Requesting a career change was easy for God, as easy as making a plant grow or making the wind blow.

As the Bible says: "Consider how the wild flowers grow. They do not labour or spin. Yet I tell you, not even Solomon in all his splendour was dressed like one of these. If that is how God clothes the grass of the field, which is here today and tomorrow is thrown into the furnace, how much more will He clothe you, O you of little faith!" (Luke 12:27)

I had to remind myself all the time about the many things that God had done for me and praise him for them, showing gratitude all the time. The frustration that I was feeling was not helping at all, and it was only turning me into an ungrateful and negative person. While I had moments of weariness and disillusionment, trusting in God was a sure formula for success. The psalmist David said, "Praise the Lord, O my soul... and forget not all his benefits. Who forgives all your sins and heals all your diseases?" (Psalm 103:1-3)

I had to remember all the time that not all desires were answered immediately or instantly, but some took some time based on the level of development I had attained. It was not only about waiting for God to fulfil my desires but also for me to learn as much as I could and reach the level of development needed for me to transcend into another job, thus making a success of the new environment with more developed skills. I also recalled the time when I was still unmarried and dating, when, although I had thought that I had the right person, it turned out not to be and the period of separation and the stress that followed were only to prepare me for my ultimate marriage to my husband. I had to develop a certain level of maturity as marriage was a lasting covenant between me and my husband, with God in the centre. I needed to be ready to assume the role of being a wife and a mother, and my emotional immaturity at that time was surely a weakness that would make it difficult for me to cope with the marriage. Looking back to when I was finally married and discussing it with my husband, I informed him that I was a better person as a result of a previous relationship I had been in. It had prepared me emotionally for the marriage, although when one enters into a union with the person one thinks is the right one, one can get lost in the relationship, only to find that it was not the divinely ordained union.

There was and is always hope in God and giving up is definitely not the answer, I realised. It was the test of my faith, believing that even though I was not experiencing the things I wanted then, with the speed at which I wanted to experience them, I could reaffirm God's faithfulness in my life by looking at past victories. It required using integrated methods that I had already learned, some to the level of mastery and others developing as I moved along.

I knew also that I wasn't alone and there were many other people who have been praying, affirming and visualising, although they hadn't yet seen the fruits of their efforts. Others gave up along the way on the methods, but that wasn't an alternative for me. I told myself: 'No matter how hard I tried, I knew that at the end I would reach my goals.' Candice had once told me that I shouldn't run away from my home following a time in my life when I was still single and trying to fill my weekends all the time by going to the mall or finding other activities to do. She had said, "You know, you need to learn to be alone in your own home and enjoy being there, because being alone doesn't have to mean loneliness." I heeded her words and learned to enjoy my own company, trusting that everything would work out at the end. If the time was not right, a time would come when success would come knocking at my door. I had seen God fill my cup to the brim and knew that when I did find my new job, it would be more than I had expected. God would surprise me and give me extras that I didn't expect, just as He did with my wedding. I had received things that I had specifically asked for, with additional gifts. God knew me better than I could ever know myself, and whatever He provided always satisfied me.

I also realised that although sometimes I didn't feel like affirming or praying, that was the same with all other areas in life. There have been reports I didn't feel like preparing, meetings I didn't feel like going to, responsibilities I didn't feel like handling, times when I didn't feel like cooking, even though we had to eat; I didn't feel like going to work sometimes, and there were many more, and these were not only my experiences but the experiences of many other people. There are times when something doesn't work out for someone but that doesn't qualify it as a failure, since we have to step out and try again and never give up hope that things will work out at the end.

15

LETTING GO AND LETTING GOD

"Be still and know that I am God."
Psalm 46:10

M y husband and I had a discussion about buying a house, and we would drive around the suburbs we wanted to live in on weekends, and sometimes look at the newspapers for houses that were on sale and that we could afford. We had different requirements, however, for the house of our dreams. I had wished for a house with a huge backyard with lots of trees and flowers, my intention being to meditate there sometimes, while my husband wanted a home with a swimming pool. I didn't like the idea of a swimming pool because I couldn't swim and the thought of having kids playing around the pool made me scared. They could fall in there and drown if they also couldn't swim or weren't being monitored, and so the swimming pool was unnecessary, according to me.

I remembered a colleague at work had told me that her son nearly drowned in a pool, and I was afraid for my own child.

My husband made me aware that I was projecting my own fears on the child and said we could take her for swimming lessons, and I could also learn how to swim. I understood his reasoning but I was still not keen. I couldn't imagine having a pool of water in my backyard; it sounded like a wasted walking space. We could use that space to plant vegetables too, I argued.

My husband also suggested that we have a dog, but even that I opposed. I've never been fond of pets, and my dad never had any. Furthermore, I was afraid of dogs. As much as we wanted a house, we couldn't agree on certain aspects. What we both knew, however, was that it had to be a three-bedroom house with a double garage. I also imagined a spare room that we could use for prayer and meditation.

Things were still not happening as far as job applications were concerned. A year had passed. I had prayed, specifying my clear and detailed requirements to God, meditated, affirmed and visualised, but nothing was coming through. I had cut pictures from the magazines of what I wanted to see and made a vision board that I mounted on the wall, but still nothing happened.

I was sitting at home one day trying to reassess my life and my needs, when I felt an innermost urge to surrender everything to God. I had done everything in my power to push the hand of God and to help Him, but nothing had transpired. *I could hand over all of my desires to God and allow Him to place me where He saw fit, although, on the other hand, where I was was probably where He wanted me to be as well,* I thought to myself.

As they say, God works in mysterious ways and all events and experiences in our lives serve a purpose. If we let go and let Him take over completely, experience has taught me that everything always works out in my favour at the end. So far I had three activities that were consuming my mind at different levels. I had choices regarding my career, the trip to India that I thought about often, and the desire for a new and perfect house.

I decided not to trouble sister Charmaine anymore, but give her time to send me a response when she was ready. I knew that I could not control the events of my life, and that all of these were beyond me, so I had to relinquish control and wait. God knew when I would go to India, and whether I should or should not; even though I had the deepest desire, I couldn't force the hand of God or make myself magically go.

I also realised that I had prayed on numerous occasions saying I surrendered all, and even sang the song, but I never really did. I never fully yielded my troubles and concerns to God.

Warren, R (2014), explained it perfectly when he said that surrendering one's life means the following:

Following God's lead without knowing where he's sending you.

Waiting for God's timing without knowing when it will come.

Expecting a miracle without knowing how God will provide.

Trusting God's purpose without understanding the circumstances.

These were the best explanations I've ever heard about surrendering, and referring back to them helped me clear my head and find alignment again.

I thought about the many scriptures I had read in the Bible, and the teachings of Jesus Christ; time after time the Bible tells us not to fear and that we would not be forsaken, but some of us don't listen. I had been afraid that if I didn't control the events of my life, perhaps others would impose on me, and if I didn't get things the way that I wanted them to be, then I would be a failure and would not enjoy life. I thought that one enjoyed life when one is in control and looking successful to the world.

I was afraid that my trip to India might not materialise and I would never discover the spiritual richness of the place as it had been described to me. I had also been very independent before I was married and did things my own way, and my ways were always right and were the only ways. I thought I could still make independent decisions in marriage, but realised that I was not alone. I did not marry myself; I was married to my husband and had to live within the arrangements of marriage. It was a covenant that I had entered into willingly and I loved and appreciated my marriage. Above all, I loved and appreciated my husband. He was always supportive and a very considerate man. It was not only my happiness that mattered, but his too.

As far as changing jobs was concerned, well, it was also a waiting game. I realised that while waiting I had to learn to enjoy what I was doing and find a balance between work and home life. I had a choice to take files home and deny my family the available time to spend with me, or I could do whatever I was able to do within the working hours of the day, knowing that the sun would rise again the following morning and I could still finish up then. Surrendering gave me freedom, inner peace and harmony, and when I made a decision to surrender, I walked around feeling joyful and light.

I thought also about the past life regression sessions that never materialised the way that I had wanted them to. I had very high expectations of the therapists and of the process. I thought I was entitled to the experience because I had asked for it, and I cherished the evidence behind the teachings, but the understanding and revelation were hidden from me. In some instances, people had shown up in my life who offered the sessions, or who knew people who offered these sessions, and I thought that was a sign that it was OK for me to undertake the experiment. Jamal and my cousin, Given, had told me at length to stop meddling with the past, but the more they tried to talk me out of it, the more I wanted to do it.

I realised with that also that I had to just let go, that I didn't have control over that knowledge. I couldn't force my subconscious mind to reveal things that it was not prepared to reveal. *'Am I really a forceful person?'* I asked myself, as I needed to answer the question.

I was invited to a women's conference in August to celebrate women's month. In South Africa, the 9th of August is a national public holiday to commemorate the day when approximately 20 000 women all over the country marched to the Union Buildings in Pretoria in 1956 to protest against having to carry passbooks. According to literature, this was a protest against the legislation that was aimed at tightening the apartheid government's control over the movement of black women in urban areas. The march culminated in the acknowledgement of women in the struggle for freedom, thereby making them equal partners in the struggle for a non-racial and non-sexist South Africa. The day is therefore referred to as Women's Day and every area, workplace, political arena and so forth generally has different events organised to mark this historical day (South African Government, 2016).

I was standing in a queue at lunch-time to fetch my food when the woman behind me said to me, "Did you hear the speeches?"

"Many women went through painful experiences in their lives, it's unbelievable!" she continued, with astonishment in her voice and a look of wonder on her face.

"Yes, you are right," I said.

"Can you remember your own life as you were growing up?" she asked.

"I really can't remember much about my childhood", I said.

"Wow, you are blessed! I believe that your childhood was wonderful and normal and that's why you can't remember anything," she said.

I was surprised by what she had said. It came so unexpectedly and I tried to figure out what had just happened.

I had tried so hard to go through sessions in order to remember my childhood, and even to go back to past lives, and here was a woman whom I had just met, who didn't even know me, telling me that I had a good life! I considered her an angel who had been sent to give me a significant message from God. What had occurred was not a coincidence, but divine intervention. I received new revelations that God communicates with us using others as well. He uses all kinds of communication at His disposal. It's up to us to notice and become aware. He also always confirms His messages by repeating them again elsewhere. I have seen this many times.

The conference took the whole day at a hotel in town. Apart from speeches, we sang and danced and celebrated our femininity. We celebrated our strength, beauty, achievements and our worth as women. It was empowering, simply being in that space and listening to other women as they encouraged us to take pride in who we are. Most of us at the conference were not even born in 1956, but it was amazing to hear and to be reminded about how women, despite their diversity, came together in unity to fight for the rights of all South African women.

I left the conference at 5 p.m. inspired, and realised that there were other important things in life besides my troubles and goals and it only required a shift of focus. I saw how God was working in my life, confirming that He was still in control. He had used yet another occasion to reach out to me and comfort me, and I had to allow Him to work His perfect plan for my life. God knew the fastest and most convenient way to realise my dreams and I didn't know these short cuts, nor could I see into the future. All I had to do was to sit, wait and trust: "…and after you have done everything, to stand." (Ephesians 6:13)

Pastor Rick Warren said that you will know that you have surrendered to God when you depend on God to work things out instead of trying to control other people, forcing your own agenda or controlling the situation. I could, therefore, also affirm that God was meeting all of my needs instead of worrying, and accept the truth that God's wisdom was always available and present, and always ready to imbue my life with understanding and a good life. God was the greatest in filling the void and the emptiness that separated me from my desires, and if anything had to happen, He would do it at the perfect time. I had been trying to do things my own way by pushing hard to get them the way I wanted them to be.

16

IT FINALLY HAPPENED...

Om Shanti

"Peace for all humankind, peace for all living and non-living beings,
peace for the universe, peace for each and every thing in this whole
cosmic manifestation."
Anonymous

I caught up with Jamal again, as I often called him whenever I needed cheering or wisdom, and he would encourage me, always saying things I wanted to hear. He understood me as he had been my mentor for quite some time. We had come a long way, and he remained my consistent friend and spiritual teacher. He asked me about the visit to India and I informed him that I hadn't heard anything from Sister Charmaine yet. He advised me that the next spiritual retreat to India was in October, and that was in two months' time. Jamal advised me to call Sister Hannah, the facilitator, instead of Charmaine, as she had done her part and was also waiting to hear from Hannah and the India office. He gave me her mobile number, as she was based in Johannesburg.

I thought, '*Cool, at least we still have two more months; that's ample time, though I need to know if I am going or not.*' I knew that I shouldn't pressurise but rather trust in God and attend to this business relaxed and calm. I took Jamal's advice and called Hannah.

"Hi, Sister Hannah, you are speaking to Kgalalelo. I got your number from Jamal," I said when she answered her mobile phone.

"Oh, hi, Kgalalelo, how are you? I've heard so much about you," she said.

"I'm doing well, thank you, but am concerned because I haven't heard anything from the centre about my motivation for the trip to India," I said.

"You didn't receive the invitation? I sent it about a week ago to the email address Charmaine gave me," she exclaimed with surprise in her voice.

"Really, I never received anything; perhaps there might have been a problem with the network, but funnily enough I have been receiving emails from my friends. Can I give you an alternative one so that you can re-send it, please?" I asked with a little bit of excitement.

"Sure, let me get a pen to write it down," she replied.

I held on for a few minutes and when she came on again I gave her my other e-mail address, and she promised to send the invitation immediately.

I spoke to Sister Hannah for a few more minutes, then hung up the telephone. Within ten minutes, I saw a prompt on my laptop screen informing me that I had mail in my other email address. I logged into my account and opened the email to find the invitation to the retreat in India. I knew from experience that when I went to London to visit Fay, I had to produce an invitation in order to qualify for a visa, and knew that this was normal procedure. I was thrilled, as I had to register online for the retreat on the link that Sister Hannah had provided me with.

Within two days, I received another email from the headquarters in India confirming my registration and was requested to book my flights and submit those details. I got in contact with

Sister Hannah, and we spoke frequently from then on, making preparations. I called Jamal and Sister Charmaine too, to inform them that I had contacted Sister Hannah and everything was on track. Sister Hannah and I communicated regularly about the best flights and the local transport we should use on arrival in India. My excitement grew every day as I began preparing myself for the trip.

We were a month away from departure, and I received updates every second day about the arrangements. I kept quiet about the trip, as I wanted everything to be finalised before I announced it to my family and friends. I began to research on the Internet about the temperature during that period and what to see in India, and was impressed and at ease about it all. I remembered also that the first time I wanted to go to India, it was challenging for me to follow a vegetarian diet as one of the requirements for the retreat, but this time I was determined, and began the first day of the month of September and went on a thirty-day fast. Surprisingly, it was quite easy to refrain from eating meat, and I found other alternatives to satisfy my desire for meat.

I put in my leave application two weeks before departure and kept in touch with Sister Hannah about the developments and other things I had to do. It was two days before the trip when she sent me another email informing me that everything was finalised and set and she would request someone to pick me up at the airport, as I was scheduled to fly to Johannesburg on Thursday afternoon, sleep over, then fly to India the next day. I was ecstatic and began thinking about the people I had to call to inform them about my trip. It felt real finally, and I gave thanks to God that another dream that I had wished to happen was really happening. I was humbled to realise that God had come through for me one more time, as He always did. I felt His amazing and unfailing love for me.

I was also grateful that my husband was allowing me to go on this trip, and that he was so selfless in knowing how important it was to me to go to India. I realised that when you have the right partner in your life, somebody who understands you and your mission in life and, above all, who knows God and always looks at things from a spiritual perspective, you can achieve so much more together. My husband and I met as a result of spiritual matters, and our spirituality is what has always grounded us and pulled us through the storms of life. I felt deep gratitude for his presence in my life and for the force that brought us together, imagining that we've always had a connection in the spiritual world. I remembered that our wedding invitation card also read that we were united together in Christ through eternity, and those words rang true for me, though I never understood them fully back then.

My anticipation grew by the day, and I had to ensure that I wrapped up what I was doing at work and put measures in place so that things would run smoothly during my absence, as I knew that I wouldn't be available on my mobile phone during that time. Wednesday came, my last day at work before going on leave. I ensured on that day that I completed all reports that were due, attended to every appointment and briefed my colleagues on what needed to be done during my absence. I couldn't wait to see the end of the day. I kept thinking about my trip and all that I would see once I got to my destination.

At lunch time, I decided to take a ride to the mall to buy minor things that I would need for the trip, and it took me quite a short time at the mall to complete my shopping. I was on my way to the office when Candice called me wanting to find out were I was. I told her that I would be in the office within ten minutes, as I was near the building. I felt satisfied as I was driving, thinking about everything I had found during shopping, and all fell into place. I had been successful in finding everything I wanted, my arrangements for the trip were perfect, and now I was preparing myself to leave, finally.

I saw the hand of God in my life yet again and believed that, as always, everything was in divine order, that God had saved me for this time and this was the appropriate and appointed time for me to take this trip, and not before. Candice came into my office just fifteen minutes after my return. I was busy reading my emails when she dropped in. She had a shopping bag in her hand and immediately I thought that she wanted to show me something that she had bought for herself. I knew my friend to be a shopaholic and was not surprised to see the bag in her hand. As she approached with a sparkle, I was staring at the shopping bag, and then she handed it to me.

"You will be away on your birthday, so I thought I should give you a birthday present in advance," she said.

I was baffled as I wasn't expecting an early birthday present. I wasn't even thinking about my birthday at that time.

"I thought I would take you out for coffee on that day, but things have changed now," she continued.

"Thank you, Candice. I wasn't expecting anything, it's quite a surprise and I appreciate it," I said.

I opened the bag to find a beautiful wooden carving of an African woman holding a bowl. I had seen this a few days ago when we had gone window shopping together at a retail store and Candice had asked me if I liked it, but I didn't know why she had asked. She knew as soon as I said yes that she would buy it for me as a birthday gift. I was happy and felt humbled by the gesture. I remembered that I had the perfect candle at home and would put it in that bowl as soon as I got home.

"Okay, then, see you, I have to go back to my office," she said preparing to leave.

"Thanks again, Candice; this is really beautiful," I replied. "I guess you beat everyone to it, especially my husband," I said laughingly.

Candice left my office, and I continued with the rest of my assignments.

I felt happy by the time I looked at my clock to find that it was time to go home. I hurried to switch off my laptop, took everything I needed at the office and headed home. My attention was fully on packing for the trip. I knew, at that moment, that this was it. I was finally going to India, and the long-anticipated trip of five years was finally happening.

Morning came; it was the 4th of October 2008 and it was time for departure. I had to take a flight to Johannesburg in the afternoon and meet up with Sister Hannah and the team, and I couldn't wait! I heard the phone ring whilst packing my suitcase; it was a text message from Sister Hannah, informing me that Laurel would pick me up at the airport and that I should look out for her grey Ford Cortina. I realised that everyone on the other side was ready for me, and that increased my anticipation even more. I cooked lunch for my family and took a bath, and, as soon as I was finished, I heard a knock on the door. It was my husband, who had come to pick me up to take me to the airport. Our daughter was at daycare. I had said my goodbyes to her in the morning. I believed that even though she was still little, she understood. She had to know that I would be away for two weeks and that daddy would be taking care of her. We left for the airport, which was ten kilometres away from home, and made it in only fifteen minutes.

It was difficult to see my husband go, as he had to go back to the office and leave me at the airport to wait for the flight. As I waved him goodbye I was still overwhelmed by gratitude that he was really allowing me to go on this trip. I went into the airport restaurant and ordered a cappuccino whilst waiting for my flight to board. I spent half an hour in the restaurant until my boarding call.

The flight to Johannesburg was an hour long and right on schedule. I spotted Laurel's car at arrivals parking bay when I walked out the exit and went to meet her. A petite Indian lady wearing a long brown skirt and a white shirt walked over to greet me as she saw me approaching. She held her hair in a bun and was short in stature like me. She looked noticeably as happy to see me as I was to see her. We had a chit-chat while packing my luggage in her boot, and then we left. The centre was only twenty minutes away from the airport, so we were there in no time. She honked the hooter when we got there, and a young lady opened the gate for us. We had come to a white double-storey house and I could see the lady on the balcony who had opened the gate with the remote.

We entered and stopped on the driveway next to the garage. Laurel climbed out of the car first and went to the door. I opened the passenger door of the car and got out, closed the door and followed Laurel with only the handbag on my hand. The suit-case was still in the car. We knocked on the door, heard people talking inside, and after a few seconds a woman opened. She greeted us with a broad smile on her face and her eyes were sparkling. You could see genuine love and kindness in her face. It was Sister Charmaine, who gave us a warm welcome with hugs. We went into the house and there was another woman in the kitchen busy cooking a vegetarian meal for later.

I wanted to meet Sister Hannah so much, but she was not there and only arrived a few minutes later. I recognised her voice when she came in and greeted me, and I immediately stood up from where I was sitting to give her a hug. She was as warm-hearted in real life as she was on the phone and had a childlike giggle.

"Come, let me show you around," Sister Hannah said as she took me into the living room and then opened the sliding door from the inside that led to the back yard of the centre. It was a beautiful sight. The yard was huge, with large naturally occur-ring oak trees all around. It gave such a feeling of tranquillity and calmness to all who came to the house. There was a small-sized elevated wooden house at the far corner of the yard that served as a secondary meditation room for those who required quietness, coupled with the view of the garden. I was in awe and knew that I would love a garden like that some day when my husband and I bought a house.

I spent the remainder of the day with everyone in the sitting room, with some moments of silent meditation at intervals. I realised that this was the norm at the centre and they had time scheduled throughout the day for meditation.

When night came, Sister Hannah showed me to my room upstairs next to her office and I retired early that evening, feeling tired.

I woke up the next day at 4:00 a.m. to the sound of the meditation music in the corridor. It was the norm in the house to meditate early in the morning at that time. I was informed that it was the purest of all hours when there was less activity in the atmosphere and all around as most people would still be resting. I covered myself with the nightgown, wore my slippers and went to the meditation room to find all the other residents of the house already sitting. I entered in silence and sat on the cushion on the floor like everyone else, remaining quiet for a thirty-minute meditation session. I went back to bed at half-past-four to finish my sleep, and woke up again at 7 a.m. It was cloudy and chilly in the morning, but that didn't bother me as I had a warm jacket and a pair of socks in my suitcase. I woke up relaxed and peaceful. I heard what sounded like someone sweeping the leaves outside, as my bed was close to the window. I went on to the balcony, opened the window to enjoy the view of the garden for a while, then went in to take a shower and ready myself. We were all set for breakfast at 8.a.m. in the kitchen, and Sister Charmaine prepared food for the road to eat again on arrival at the airport.

We left towards noon, and two other ladies, who were also going with us to the retreat in India, joined us at the airport, so we were five ladies in all, including Sister Hannah. I was very comfortable with everyone and looking forward to this trip, although the plane was scheduled to leave only at 3 p.m. So we spent time getting to know each other at the airport until such time as we had to proceed to the boarding gates. There were few people travelling to Mumbai on that day and so the plane was not full when we got in; there were plenty of open seats for us to move around, and the soft instrumental music was playing in the background, eastern-style, just perfect for a long flight. I settled in at one of the window seats and thanked God again for the wonderful moment I was enjoying and the knowledge that I was heading for India. The excitement of the moment filled me and, even though the food had been prepared by Sister Charmaine, I couldn't eat it.

Our flight to Dubai took seven hours, and then we took a connecting flight to India two hours later. We could walk and relax our legs while waiting for the next flight to Mumbai. It was not an exhausting flight, however, considering that there was movement on the plane as we were fewer passengers and, compared to the eleven-hour direct flight to London that I took a few years ago, this was much better. Two hours passed quickly before we had to board again for India. We flew two hours and forty minutes from Dubai to Mumbai. This was approximately a twelve-hour trip in all, and I felt exhausted when we arrived at Mumbai airport; that flight seemed long for some weird reason and I dozed off every now and then. When the plane finally came to a standstill, I praised God that we had arrived safe and sound and were finally in India.

We left the plane and approached customs, where I handed my passport to the customs official, who looked at the picture on the passport, then looked at me, looked again at the photo, and looked at me again for the second time. I wondered why he was looking at me that much, and figured that it might have been that my hairstyle looked different to the photo on the passport, so he needed to authenticate.

I was anxious to get to the other side, the actual place, and when the customs official handed me the passport, I rushed to join my companions as I was the last in the queue. We were fortunate to find our Indian hosts waiting for us at the taxi rank. They knew Sister Hannah and so they recognised each other, and walked over to meet us. "Om Shanti," they greeted meaning 'I am a peaceful soul' or 'We are peaceful souls' or 'We come in peace'. We greeted the same way too and followed the sisters. It was very hot and humid outside as we walked out of the airport. I had a light jacket on and soon took it off as I couldn't stand the heat. The weather reminded me of Durban back home in South Africa, and felt much the same, while, coming from a very dry area, the humidity and the heat were overwhelming to us. I needed to call home before leaving the airport to inform my husband that I had arrived safe and sound, and I was afforded the opportunity to use the public phone. The entire group decided there and then also to call their families to inform them of their arrival.

When we were done, we all took a taxi to the local centre in Mumbai to refresh. This was the beginning of my spiritual rendezvous in India. All I've ever known from the group was genuine love and kindness, and that is the kind of treatment and welcome we received there. It was not unusual at all, I was used to it, appreciated it and cherished it very much, and hence I was so drawn to spending time with Jamal and the entire Brahma Kumaris.

We left the centre in Mumbai that evening and took a train to Mount Abu in Rajasthan. We settled comfortably into our compartment that we shared with two other people who were travelling the same way. The train was full and, as I looked out the window, I saw people young and old begging for money at the station, where I heard the chant, "Rupee, rupee, rupee". They asked whoever cared to listen, and some would give a coin while others just passed them by and even scolded them.

I was filled with compassion, knowing that the situation was not unique. In South Africa, where I came from, we had thousands of people who still lived in poverty and in fact, this is the case across the continent of Africa.

I settled myself and wrapped myself up in a light blanket as it was getting dark and breezy, and I thought that this was going to be an experience I would remember forever. The train left the station slowly and steadily increased speed with a typical chugging sound. It whistled in the twilight and I closed the window shade as there was not much to see outside any more after sunset. Sister Charmaine had baked a fruitcake for us for the road and we unwrapped the foil and indulged ourselves. It was an overnight voyage, and so three hours into the journey I snuggled on to the top bench and dozed off.

I rose up in the morning when I felt the warmth of sunlight on my face. I stretched my legs, yawned, opened my eyes and got up. We were ten minutes from Mount Abu. I folded my blanket, climbed off the bench and put my shoes on as we prepared to disembark. We had arrived at the hometown headquarters of the Brahma Kumaris World Spiritual University. Brothers from campus had arrived to fetch us as they knew the time of the train's arrival.

At the headquarters everyone was happy to see us, and people had come from all over the world to be part of the spiritual retreat. We were all tired and were ushered to the residential area where rooms were allocated for all of us to settle in and prepare for the welcoming ceremony in the evening. We spent the entire day touring the campus, and went into the village to buy supplies. When evening came we all convened at the biggest lecture hall on campus. We literally had representatives from all over the world and, like us, they had come in groups of four and a coordinator, as that was the quota allowed for each country for the purpose of the smooth management and running of the retreat. The evening event was magical, with Indian dance choreographies from groups around Rajasthan province and Delhi.

It was a night of festivity and fun as the hosts ensured that we truly felt comfortable and welcomed. We left the lecture hall at 10 p.m. to go to our rooms and prepare for the following day's schedule. We all knew that 4 a.m. was scheduled for meditation, which was held in the same lecture hall. I identified with that routine as I had experienced it in Johannesburg and Jamal too practised it. We would go to meditation at that time in the morning for thirty minutes, then go back to the residential area either to sleep until breakfast or just stay awake and have coffee in the residence kitchen.

The entire week at the spiritual academy consisted of meditation experiences and trips to the temples, the park and the mountain for silent morning walks, saturating ourselves in the beauty of nature. We also visited the village quite often, meeting the community during leisure time. Each moment was amazing and heavenly. Lectures were arranged, as well as group sessions, to discuss the practice of meditation and how to integrate this in our everyday lives. Each day, with each activity, brought joy to my heart and complete peace. I was going to go home at the end of the week to enjoy my life with my family and continue to feel and express gratitude each and every day which, I felt, was my religion. I felt content and happy that this had happened. October the 8th was my birthday and I was still in India. On that day, a cake was arranged from the kitchen for all guests who had birthdays in October. It was a beautiful occasion as all five of us held the knife together to cut the heart-shaped cake. There was so much love and unity, the kind you would imagine in heaven, to my limited knowledge.

I still had three more days before going back home when I received an email from my husband that had been forwarded to him from my workplace. I felt upset as everyone knew that I was on leave and I didn't wish to be disturbed or even think about work. It was then that I decided to go to the meditation room, sit in silence and connect with God. When I got up, I went to the phone office and called my husband. It was refreshing to hear his voice. I informed him about my whereabouts and what we were doing and wanted to know about my baby. A few minutes after the love talk we spoke about the email from work, and I explained to him that it distracted me, whereupon he informed me that it was not work that was stealing my peace, but I was stealing my own peace by allowing work to upset me. He also said that it showed that I still had issues to work on to ensure that peace was second nature to me, no matter what happened or who said what to me.

So I had to receive that email for me to look inside myself for parts that still needed healing. I left the phone booth feeling thankful for my husband's words, as they were comforting and encouraging and made me realise that, even though I was in the atmosphere of peace and surrounded by that vibration at the academy, I still had to go home and work on ensuring that I enjoyed the peace in my everyday life, too.

We left the spiritual academy on Sunday morning and, as much as I had a fabulous time there, I was looking forward to going home and being with my family. I had only one wish when I left, and that was to carry the peaceful vibration I had experienced there with me home and live harmoniously each and every moment of my life. I knew that it was upon me, though, that I had to make the effort to remember all that I had experienced there. It didn't seem like a difficult thing to do, but I knew that going home and being exposed to the buzz of everyday life that I didn't have in India posed a different challenge; a test, however, I was willing to take on.

I knew, through various spiritual teachings, that I needed my circumstances in order to grow. I needed the people who surrounded me, the frustration that I had left before I departed for India, the challenges of my job and all that was happening in my life in order to expand, develop and advance. Some people would say 'no pain, no gain'. I guess, when I got home, those words rang true for me. As much as I wanted the experience of meditation in my life on a daily basis, that meant that I had to get up early every morning in order to have my moments of silence; there was no sister or brother next to me to hold my hand. I had myself and I was the only person who could make this work, who could help me grow in the direction that I wanted to go and, to me, there was no better direction than a spiritually focused one. I was determined to live each and every day making an effort, and was willing to try methods that I hadn't tried before in order to open myself up. I had learned a great deal in India in the midst of the experts, and they could only do what they had done for me in that period. The rest was up to me.

Our trip to the airport in Ahmedabad by bus took six hours, and we all had to exercise patience. The spiritual academy was on a mountain top and going down by bus took many twists and turns. As the bus swerved, we hung on to our seats tightly; I felt nauseous and wanted to throw up, until all of a sudden I began to feel weak and couldn't breathe. Carol was sitting next to me and, realising that I was suffering from shortness of breath, opened the window and gave me a paper bag to use in case I threw up. It certainly was not a smooth ride and I couldn't wait to reach a flatter surface. I leaned on Carol for support and fell asleep. I woke up when we reached Ahmedabad airport, where we took a flight to Mumbai. Unlike the adventure of taking the train when we first arrived, we were all eager to go home and opted for the bus instead.

I arrived home on Monday evening. My husband and daughter were at the airport, patiently awaiting my return. I was sitting on the plane in anticipation, and the hour-long flight from Johannesburg to Bloemfontein seemed like decades. I couldn't wait to see the joy in their eyes when they saw me, too. On arrival I rushed to get my huge suitcase. I had to pay an extra twenty-six rand at the airport as I had exceeded the required weight on local flights; that didn't bother me, however, as I had brought some goodies from India for my loved ones and I knew they would appreciate them. I wheeled my suitcase out of the arrival door, and there were my husband and child; one look at them brought an overwhelming feeling of gladness, love and appreciation for them. I couldn't wait for lots of hugs and kisses, and that was exactly what I got.

I still had four more days before I returned to work, and we made plans to visit my parents in Klerksdorp. I had yet another mission to fulfil, and that was to ask my parents why we had had to move from Vaal Reefs to Mafikeng. I had never bothered to ask all those years but, after twenty-five years, I felt that it was time. I was curious to know, and I wanted to go home and do exactly that - ask. We headed for Klerksdorp on Friday, with the intention of sleeping over and returning the following day. I was happy that my little brother and his wife would be at home as well, so that I could share my story with everyone at home. We arrived in the afternoon; my mother was at work, and we were expecting her in the evening at around half-past-seven. My father asked my husband and me to go and fetch her to surprise her. I knew she would be happy to see us, and I was longing to see her, too. For a few moments, thinking about it, I felt like a baby longing for the breast milk and its mother's cuddling. I realised that I was missing her and that I hadn't seen her for a few months.

Being at home with my family was always restorative. I felt that some parts of my soul needed to be there, even though I didn't say or do anything. Seeing my family soothed wounds in my heart, and filled the emptiness that I didn't know existed. The act of going home was, therefore, just enough for my soul; seeing the family laugh and hearing everyone's voice as we sat together outside on the veranda was calming and made me feel happy and blissful. I had the opportunity that afternoon to speak to my father, as I had told him before we left that I needed to talk to him, and in particular needed the full story that symbolised the Israelites leaving Egypt to go to the perceived promised land.

My father, husband and I settled on the three garden chairs on the veranda for the inevitable conversation, as I asked my father to detail for me the reasons for our leaving. The reason was not to find out if life would have been better for us had we stayed; I just wanted to understand for myself. Considering all its challenges and circumstances that made me angry sometimes, I was grateful that we had moved to Mafikeng, for I had learnt so many things there and the place surely shaped my character, but I knew that it had been unpleasant for my mother; she never quite felt at home there, and the place also turned against my father, but I didn't know his side of the story and wanted to find out.

"Your uncle had approached me one day, and told me that there were lucrative job opportunities in Mafikeng and felt that I should go for it, move back home and work there," my father said. My uncle lived in Magogoe village in Mafikeng with his family.

"At that time, it really looked as if I would make a better life for my family, as the department that your uncle introduced me to was interested in employing me, and it all sounded promising. As a result, I then decided to move but, as soon as I got there, I was told that the department wouldn't be hiring any more. I was devastated and had to aggressively look for a job quickly, as we didn't have a place to stay."

I remembered, as my father was speaking that, when we arrived in Mafikeng, we had stayed with our uncle and his family for a while before we moved to the house that I was raised in, approximately eighteen kilometres away. I sat there with my notebook, not wanting to miss anything, and listening carefully to my father's words.

"I soon found a job, and it was a great job, indeed one which I enjoyed very much. I was a deputy director for training, and this job gave me the opportunity to do much and to travel. I felt that I was growing and could see that I could go far with this job, but something went wrong. Your uncle and I were accused of doing things that we didn't have anything to do with, just because our father was a very influential politician. I guess our father was unpopular in the stream of politics, so the head of the department ensured that he found something trivial to pin us down with in a bid to remove us from the system, and so we were both dismissed."

My father went on to tell me that he hadn't been able to stay in Mafikeng during that time, as he needed to make a living and support his family, and he had turned to the district that had been his and my mother's home for a long time, and developed a successful teaching career there; that's when he applied for a teaching position in Klerksdorp again, and moved to build a life and a home for us. I think that was the best move for us, as I had never seen my mother so happy.

We went back home on the morning of the following day, Saturday. I was elated that I had closure on that chapter of my life. I knew that my life had many chapters that needed closure and healing, but also knew that I had to take it one step at a time as everything always happened at the right time. I gave thanks to God for having created that particular opportunity which had come at the right time just after a sabbatical. I went back to work on Monday, wearing a white outfit, remembering my time in India and seeking to reconnect and spread the light in that environment. On the same day, I decided to go to the doctor as I wasn't feeling well. It was exactly the same feeling I had felt when I was in the bus to Ahmedabad airport in India. I was feeling nauseous, dizzy and weak and couldn't understand what the problem was this time, as then I had assumed it had been because of the altitude, due to the road which kept swerving up and down the mountain. I had also been reading at that time, and Carol reckoned that had also contributed to my road sickness.

I made an appointment to see the doctor at 10:15 a.m. and

left at ten o' clock as it was within walking distance. My regular doctor was not there for that week, and her partner was the only one who could see me. I arrived at the doctor's room, not particularly worried about anything, but wanting to get to the bottom of my illness. It had been nine days since I had been feeling awful and weak, and I couldn't blame the altitude and the bus any more. I was home, on flat ground. It was routine for the doctor to do a urine test whenever I consulted just to see if she could pick up anything sinister. To my delight, she lifted the reader and said, "Congratulations; you are pregnant!"

Wow, a trip to India and now I was pregnant, I thought. I was so happy to hear the news of my pregnancy. Everything was like a dream. I was still reeling from the excitement of having been to India, and now more exciting news. I knew that this was an act of God, who had been faithful to me all these years and had never failed me, and now He was showering me with blessing after blessing. I left the surgery with excitement, and couldn't wait to break the news to my husband. On my way back to work I said a silent prayer to thank God for the miracles and wonders of my life. My life has been a huge adventure right from the beginning, and all of it has been exciting and challenging at the same time.

I had been guided and led all the days of my life, and at times I couldn't see where I was going, but I always ended up at the right places, making the right choices, with good things just falling into my lap. I knew that I was reaping good rewards, and God had been my radar all the years of my life. All that had happened to me had to happen for my good. Even the pain that I felt and the frustrations, all have been good and were paving a way for more goodness in my life. I knew that in some instances I didn't even have to ask much, or lift a finger, that things would just fall into place. I also attributed everything to the positive outlook that I've always had and the everyday gratitude that brought more things for me to be grateful for.

17

What Was the Fuss All About?

"Free your mind and be in the flow of life's ups and downs. Be accepting of wherever you are on your journey."
Karon Waddell

The study of the mind process is one of the most valuable studies that I came to appreciate and love as far as spirituality is concerned. I have been introduced to lessons on the different faculties of the mind and what the mind could do for me, how to tap into it and reap the benefits. I have learned that knowing how the mind works liberates us, as we begin to live consciously. The awareness of our thoughts at every moment brings a sense of control over our lives. We begin to awaken, as the Bhuddists put it. We rise from the deep soul sleep and the barriers are lifted. In the Bible, the message is depicted by Paul when he was blinded on the road to Damascus to persecute Christians. When he finally recovered his eyesight the Bible recorded that something like scales fell from his eyes, and he was baptised and preached the gospel of Jesus Christ.

When we become aware of who we really are, as souls, and the gift of the mind we have been given, we start living the kind of life we were meant to live. Once we understand our thoughts, we begin to transcend and realise that above the mind there is power that supersedes ordinary thinking and that is the presence of God. The mind therefore becomes the instrument one can use in order to merge with the unlimited power and the presence of God. As we think thoughts, some generate intense emotions that are joyful, whereas others bring fear and worry. I've experienced that we all want to feel joyful all the time because it is the nature of joy to want to share itself and rub off on anyone who comes into contact with it. This is a wonderful space to be in, but only if we think good and wholesome thoughts.

My schooling years brought about a combination of thoughts, wondrous and fearful, and all of these carved my life's experiences and I begun a long journey of soul-searching and finding meaning and purpose that ensued later in life. Perhaps we come with different manuals on earth, and even our parents do the best that they can with the limited knowledge they have. They can't live the experiences for us, nor think for us as we develop.

I was born in one part of the province and raised in another, and my birth and nurturing were great and innocent. Life, however, was filled with rough patches and experiences that only I had to go through, and no one else. I felt as if I had been thrown into the world and left there to fend for myself.

As I matured, I discovered that this was not only my story, but that most souls have passed through the same experiences one way or the other. It might not have been as a result of the things I went through, but there were other issues that dampened my optimism and enthusiasm for life. I also found comfort in the knowledge that I was not alone.

Looking back to that time, I realised how those childhood experiences had affected my life, and knew that my children would have their own experiences as well. I realise that I wouldn't be able to hide them from the world nor keep them away from any experience, but I could do my part in educating them about the things that I never received education on when I was growing up. I could watch them grow, kiss their wounds when they fell, and hug them whenever they needed it, but I wouldn't be able to live their lives for them. Perhaps all that happened to me was part of my curriculum here on earth and they too would have their own, but they would be in the state of knowing. I had to go through my own set of experiences in order to grow and progress in my spiritual journey. In the process, I had to let go as well.

If only I had known that I was on a chosen journey, a chosen stage play and in a chosen body, I would have remembered there and then the reason for my being. However, how could I have remembered my purpose of being at such an early stage? Perhaps there are those incredible souls who have evolved greatly and have had glimpses of the unfolding of their lives. I guess I was not one of those souls. I was one who was meant to gradually develop and grow through it all, experience all forms of fear and grow through them.

I felt treated, to a degree, like a decent human being when I got to high school and subsequently university, was liked by my peers, and I fitted in.

At university, the responsibility for our education was left with us; we had to discipline ourselves to submit our work on time and to study on our own. I had poured all of my energy into my education to finally make it, and I did. My thoughts were, therefore, invested in my education and the desire to live a better life for myself as soon as I had completed my degree.

Then came marriage and I realised that marriage was also another stage that requires constant effort. People have evolved over the centuries, and many teachings regarding marriage as well are at our disposal through spiritual channels, psychological routes, and many books and writings. There are countless books written by men and women of God on the subject of marriage and how people should conduct themselves in their marriages. Seminars are being held all around the world to help people handle their marriages better and to live in harmony with each other and, despite what could be said about marriage, people still believe in the institution of marriage and what it represents. Although people dispute and attack marriage, it doesn't stop people from getting married, especially young people. I believed in marriage, even when Mama Dixie had felt I was inviting trouble in my life.

I've had my great moments and not so great moments too. I guess God never promised sunshine without rain, but I still believe in marriage. I believe that relationships or marriages can be used as a platform for spiritual practice, growth and development. In fact, you can learn more about yourself in your relationship with your partner than on your own. No one says that it would be easy to live with another human being from a different background, culture and creed. In fact, it can be very challenging. I have been fortunate to be married to a man who supports me and really wants to see me grow, and that is incredible. It made me see the importance of the right foundation to marriage, and that is one based on spiritual values and the support of loved ones.

Looking at my quest to learn about past lives and the minimal results I had achieved so far, I appreciated that I had been inaugurated into God's grace before I even embarked on any teaching, I was sealed into grace and it was enough. In 2 Corinthians 12:9 Jesus said, "My grace is sufficient for you, for my power is made perfect in weakness." I had chosen the path of grace a long time ago and was established into the flock of Christ. I heard His voice the very first time He called and I jumped in. It became superfluous therefore for me to keep on chasing the experiences that continually eluded me no matter how hard I tried. I was familiar with the voice of Jesus, and it was the only voice that was ingrained inside my mind and that was evident also in my sleep state. Whenever I had nightmares and someone was chasing me in a dream or sought to harm me, I called the name of Jesus in my sleep all the time no matter what I was doing or learning at any point in time. It was automatic and He rescued

244

me. This was the only name that came to mind even in the sleep state and I knew that was the only name I could hang on to and feel safe with. I understood what grace meant as I listened to more sermons by different preachers, that indeed my sins were forgiven and still are, past, present and future. I needn't worry about what to fix or rectify in my past, even if there were past lives, the experiences were all forgiven two thousand years ago on the cross. Believing this way and sealing myself in the knowledge of grace I found was the easiest thing I could do for myself. It offered comfort, and faith was the only thing that was required.

On the other hand, healing the mind with other techniques served me in different ways too, and my observation was that many people go for prayer, often for the same things, without doing the work. They believe that as they leave the altar after prayer, depression, for instance, would have disappeared. There are instances where that did occur, but the clergyman would confirm or tell you that at times there is more that is required to heal the innermost chambers of the heart or the mind. Counselling sometimes is required, meaning some technique is required to peel the onion and get to the compartments that have been closed up. People do suppress their emotions and tough experiences; we are not robots but human beings, and we are being something, we are becoming and transforming into the image and likeness of God, our original state. We are all on the journey home, meaning our natural state before the fall of man from grace, and it takes effort sometimes to align ourselves with that original state which is the presence of God, but once we are aligned, then everything is easy and effortless, life becomes good again and we live in a state of bliss, but once we lose our way home, we begin to suffer again, walk in the maze, fall and are bruised until we find the way again. Like prodigal sons, God always welcomes His children home no matter how often they fall.

The Brahma Kumaris taught me that the most important journey that one could ever take in life was the journey within. The process of going within was simply the journey of disconnecting with harmful habits and connecting with innate spiritual resources. I always saw resonance in my spiritual path; that most humans seek to connect with a higher power no matter what we understand that power to be.

The Brahma Kumaris describes God as 'the perfect and constant embodiment of all virtues, powers and values, and that He is the unconditionally loving Father of all souls, irrespective of their religion, gender or culture'. They consider 'God's purpose to be the spiritual re-awakening of humanity and the removal of sorrow, evil and negativity'. (Brahma Kumaris, 2016)

I observed that all components in all religions' descriptions of God are contained in these narratives.

As people, too, we place too many expectations on the things that we want to see. Sometimes we don't really understand the concept of surrendering. I still at times confuse surrendering with giving up. I realised in my own life that when I surrender I am peaceful and calm, whereas when I give up there is a sense of frustration. My body even loses tenseness and I accept what is without seeking to change it or fight it, especially people. I seek not to change anyone and even if I require a changed behaviour from another, there is no exasperation. I often felt that when I surrendered, I didn't suffer at all and the world ceased the fight against me. All of a sudden things begin to take care of themselves and others that I had been at loggerheads with suddenly change their behaviour towards me.

The popular hymn goes:
All to Jesus I surrender,
All to Him I freely give;
I will ever love and trust Him,
In His presence daily live.
I surrender all,
I surrender all.
All to Thee, my blessed Saviour,
I surrender all.

I've always sung it at the top of my lungs, and the most wonderful thing about singing to God is that it is often not a performance, you just sing with the natural voice that He has given you, but I came to learn that surrendering was more than just saying the words; you need to know that you have surrendered for sure, and not revisit your troubles, nor take back your worries and pain. We also want to tell God what to do and how to do it and we never listen to the whisper of His guidance. There are dozens of ways in which God communicates with us and we fail to listen because we are expecting other forms of communication.

This work never ends and, wherever a person goes, there are lessons to learn or remember. Our growth is never complete. We can never say that we have arrived, since when you think you have arrived, another journey begins. I have been on many expeditions in my life and, when one was completed, another commenced. Some have been exciting and full of fun and some were dreadful but I was able to pull through at every stop. I never appreciated some of the humps though; being mocked about any part of my being, for instance, when I was growing up, and this journey and chapter hadn't really been closed as I would feel offended when I heard others mocking other people, and especially when kids were mocked.

My problem with weight has never ended, but has been better controlled by safe means and moderate exercise.

I have a library of books in my house. New thought, metaphysics, Christian and all have contributed and still contribute to my growth, depending on what I wish to learn or remember, and they keep me focused all the time. Nobody said that life will be easy, but again one cannot struggle for the rest of one's life as we have to keep on making an effort. We are told that God created us for His enjoyment and if we are extensions of God, it means we are God and God is the never-ending state of pure bliss.

I believe in this state of pure bliss and my connection with God is the only thing that makes sense to me, and when I am not connected, I feel disturbed and frightened and think about the most outrageous things. I know, whenever I feel scared, that I need to hand over to God completely, but sometimes I struggle to because the world does things in a particular way and it is easier to do what others do.

The second pregnancy came at the perfect time to help me refocus on other things instead of wanting things to go my own way, and that's how God has saved me from myself. He always gave me something else which is fulfilling to change the focus of my attention so that I might not hurt myself even more.

I know as well that even my next adventure will be divinely orchestrated, as everything else has been in my life.

* * * * * * *

I humble myself before You, God, knowing that You are the Creator of all. Teach me to be still and know that You are God; teach me Your ways that I may constantly walk in Your Path, Amen.

LIST OF REFERENCES

Books

Bays B. (1999), *The Journey*. London: Harper Collins Publishers.

Byrne R. (2006), *The Secret*. Great Britain: Simon & Schuster UK Ltd.

Hay L. (1984). *You can heal your life*. South Africa by arrangement with Hay House, Inc.: Paradigm Press, CC.

Jones H. M.D. (1998). *"Doctor, What's the Alternative?"* London: Hodder and Stoughton.

O'Donnell K. (1987). *New Beginnings*. UK: Brahma Kumaris Raja Yoga Centres Inc.

Prophet E.C. (1997). *Access the Power of Your Higher Self*. USA: Summit Publications, Inc.

New International Version, Holy Bible. (2005). Cape Town: Struik Christian Books.

Wales, S. (2001). *Standing on the Promises*. USA: Multonmah Publishers, Inc.

Weiss, B.L. M.D. (1988). *Many Lives, Many Masters*. USA: Simon & Schuster, Inc.

Internet

Eddie Seanan, www.thepowerwithinus.co.za/2015/06/26/the-peace-mantra-om-shanti-om/. Ascension Movement, Raising Consciousness. The peace mantra: Om Shanti.

Warren R. (2014). *Surrender: Let Go and Let God Work.* (Online). Available at: http://pastorrick.com/devotional/english/surrender-let-go-and-let-god-work-_456.

Brahma Kumaris. (2016). (Online). Available at:www.brahmakumaris.org.

South African Government. (2016). *Women's Month 2015.* (Online). Available at: http://www.gov.za/womens-month-1-31-aug-2015.

The International Centre of Reiki Training (1990-1996) (Online) Available at:
http://www.reiki.org/faq/whatisreiki.html.

Wiley J. 2016, Understanding the Principles of Feng-shui Available Online at: www.dummies.com/how-to/content/understanding-the-principles-of-**feng-shui**.html.

Quotes

A Z Quotes. *Harriet Martineau.* (Online). Available at: http://www.azquotes.com/quote/837715.

Bhakti Breakfast Club. (Online). Available at: http://www.bhaktibreakfastclub.com/mantraglossary55.

Brainyquotes. 2001-2016. (Online). Available at:
www.brainyquote.com/quotes/quotes/n/novakdjoko428255.
html.

Brainyquotes. 2001-2016. (Online). Available at: www.
brainyquote.com/quotes/quotes/m/michaeldel173359.html.

Brainyquotes. 2001-2016. (Online). Available at: http://www.
brainyquote.com/quotes/quotes/c/confucius140908.html.

Daily Inspirational Quotes. (2016). Tony Gaskins. (Online).
Available at: http://www.dailyinspirationalquotes.
in/2016/02/24/trust-the-process-your-time-is-coming-just-
do-the-work-and-the-results-will-handle-themselves-tony-
gaskins/.

EyeOpenerQuotes. (2016). *Memorable Moments*. (Online).
Available at: www.eyeopenerquotes.com.

Fine R.G. (2013). *Inspirational Quotes*. (Online). Available at:
www.eyeopenerquotes.com › Memorable Moments.

http://lifeasahuman.com/2013/just-saying-quotations/
inspirational-quotes-by-randi-g-fine/.

Goodreads Inc. 2016. *Martin Luther King, Jr.* (Online). Available
at: www.goodreads.com/.../7847-intelligence-plus-character-
that-is-the-goal-of-true-education.

Goodreads Inc. 2016. *Benjamin Spock.* (Online). Available at:
http://www.goodreads.com/quotes/4422-trust-yourself-you-
know-more-than-you-think-you-do.

Goodreads Inc. 2016. *Karon Waddell.* (Online). https://www.

goodreads.com/author/quotes/15107446.Karon_Waddell.
Louisearmstrong.com. 2016. (Online). Available at: http://
www.louise-armstrong.com/when-you-fear-your-struggles-
your-struggles-consume-you-when-you-face-your-struggles-
you-overcome-them/.

https://www.flickr.com/photos/ranveig/14858928710.

www.ingramcontent.com/pod-product-compliance
Lightning Source LLC
Chambersburg PA
CBHW031532040426
42445CB00010B/496